Walk Your Own Camino

Themes and Variations along the
Camino de Santiago

DIANNE HOMAN

To Reinhard, who walks with me.

CONTENTS

ACKNOWLEDGMENTS

Many thanks to Jim for careful reading and
detailed comments.

And to Marie, for good advice and encouragement.

To Keara, for helping to get it out there.

And to the many pilgrims who inspired the stories
in this book.

INTRODUCTION

The Walking Camino

Well of course it's a walking camino, you might say – unless you are one of those who bike the trail. And walking is something most of us take for granted. Heck, we humans generally start doing it around our first birthdays. But the camino has a way of shaking things up – your body, your mind, your spirit, everything you've ever taken for granted. It's a gentle shake, nothing to get upset about. But the result is that you and you and you and I all mean something different when we say the words "walking camino."

For instance, you, the retired sisters from Vermont and Illinois, see the walking in small increments for a very good reason. Every step hurts. At the end of a day of slow trudging, you lie down for a long time on your pre-booked lower bunks in an albergue. That's where you are when I meet you. I listen to your conversation as you study the guidebook, express nervousness about the elevation gains and losses on tomorrow's stretch of trail, calculate how far

1

you'll be able to go, and determine which accommodation will suit your many needs best. You pull out your phone to make reservations and arrange for the baggage-handling service to pick up and deliver your backpacks. When we start to talk, you tell me that you are only walking short sections of the camino. The rest will be covered by taxi or bus.

The walking is hard on you. It's almost like an enemy you have to face. You complain that the Sheen / Estevez movie, "The Way", didn't show how much pain pilgrims endure. It didn't include scenes of blister-popping and foot-bandaging. You know the story was about other issues, big emotional issues, but it still bugs you that your battles weren't portrayed in the film.

I wonder, to myself, why the two of you are doing the trail. Maybe you wonder the same thing. I imagine one of you having had a dream – a dream big enough to send you across the Atlantic Ocean. Do you remember, sister? It was when you were twenty. You were sleeping in a tent for the first, and only, time in your life. You had started out shivering and feeling miserable until someone, you don't remember who, lent you a good sleeping bag.

As you settled into a grateful and warm sleep, you saw yourself walking on horizontal shafts of gold sunlight – gliding actually – skating from beam to beam toward something wondrous, toward perfection. You could have gone on forever. When you woke in the morning, you stayed very still for a long time, holding on to the vision. You called it a "joy dream." When you got home from the camping trip, you told your sister about it, and she wrote a song inspired by the images. Her song was the hit of the coffee house circuit for a while. Maybe the dream and the song were a bridge to the camino. Maybe that's why the two of you are here.

I run into you, the tall smiling man from London, England, almost every day for the first couple of weeks on the camino. I never walk with you though, because your pace is so much faster than mine. You make it look effortless.

One day, I pass by as you're eating lunch at an outdoor table and ask if you will be stopping for the night in Arcahueja. You say that you'll continue on into León; it's only an extra eight kilometers.

"Only?" I say.

"Yeah, just another hour and a half," you reply.

I laugh and say there's no way I can walk five kilometers an hour with a heavy pack on my back, and you say you're trying to work up to six. At that I wave and say goodbye but feel sad that you'll probably be at least eight kilometers ahead of me for the rest of the camino, and I won't see you again.

I can picture you as a boy playing with other kids. They climb trees, make monkey sounds, and scratch their armpits. Or they gallop across lawns, slapping the sides of their thighs and whinnying to each other. You smile your gentle smile and move your own way, like a giraffe on the wide savannah, so quiet, so graceful, so effortless. You had a small wooden carving of a giraffe that you kept always in your right pants pocket. When you touched it, it gave you power.

On one of those days before León, you told me you were recently divorced. You missed living with your kids and you hated being in a small lonely apartment. I think the giraffe led you to this, your walking camino – to give you power again.

And you, my new friend from Edmonton, Alberta. You, your husband and I had dinner together so many evenings. I'm remembering our last afternoon in Villafranco del Bierzo, where you would end your camino. The three of us are sitting in the sunshine on the plaza, and your husband says this is what he'll miss the most about the camino -- enjoying a cool drink, watching other peregrinos arrive in town and having the chance to reconnect. "We're like different-colored threads criss-crossing and braiding," he says. You are quiet for a moment, then say you will miss the walking. We all get kind of choked up at that.

You just retired from a well-paid administrative assistant job. You can't believe you sat in an office for thirty years. You remember being six and spinning barefoot in the middle of your yard. The neighbor kids laughed when you got dizzy and fell down. Then you stopped getting dizzy, and the kids stopped laughing. They were in awe, at first, that you could keep turning and turning, but then they got bored and left. You kept going. You had found the stillness at the center, and it was the best place of all.

You found it again as a young teen, riding your bike fast, ten times around the block clockwise and ten times counter-clockwise. You found it again at university, running track.

During your working years, you stayed in shape by going to the gym after work, and you pretty much forgot about, or gave up as a thing of youth, that place of peace at the center of movement.

But I know you found it again on the camino, because after you said you would miss the walking, you stood up, walked to the middle of the square, stretched out your arms, and turned around one time slowly, your face as open as the sky.

I ask myself what was my bridge to the camino, and one memory comes immediately to mind. I was seventeen and in a deep seventeen-year-old funk. I'd taken to spending evenings in any room where other members of my family weren't, without the lights on, watching it get dark.

One hot summer day, black clouds brought night early. You can't even call what came next "rain." It was a deluge. Every drop that hit the ground bounced back up at least a foot. The roof thundered so loudly under the onslaught, I had to raise my voice to ask my dad if I could borrow his raincoat.

It was knee-length on him, which meant it reached mid-calf on me. It had a big hood and sleeves that covered my hands. I fastened it all the way up, slipped on my rubber flip-flops, and headed out the door. I wanted the rain to beat me up or to make me more miserable or to convince me how little I mattered in the grand scheme of things.

Mattering mattered to my teenage self. I wanted boys to look at me. I wanted to be friends with the cool girls. I wanted something about me to be special that had nothing to do with getting good grades in school or winning the high-jump contest in gym.

That storm baptized me as special, all right, but it had nothing to do with other people and whether they noticed me or not. Like a vengeful god, the rain was a force to be reckoned with, and there I was out in it – reckoning. Me, alone. No one else was crazy enough to be out there that night. My ears filled with the rapid-fire hammering of drops against the raincoat material and the sound of my own breathing – sucked in and blown out like a boxer's. My vision blurred with house lights and streetlights broken up into a beaded crystal curtain. The smell of ozone and wet asphalt was delicious enough to stick out my tongue and lick my lips for. My feet were washed and blessed and washed again by splashes of cold, cool and warm, depending on whether the rain was rebounding off the grass, the sidewalk or the street.

Dry and secure inside the raincoat, I could not even remember what I'd been so bummed out about. I kept walking and kicking puddles and dancing in the rain like Gene Kelly until the storm hushed to a whisper. I couldn't have put it into words at the time, but I learned something big --that mattering is not ego-centric. What matters is to be out walking and noticing and being one who's crazy enough to do things. Things like going out in storms. Things like hiking the camino.

We peregrinos are there together, in body, mind and spirit, and we're shaking up the things we've always taken for granted. Your stories, impressions, memories and experiences weave together to form what you will call "your camino." And as we walk and talk, some colorful threads of our stories will be joined. You and you and you become part of my camino, and I become part of yours.

THE HISTORICAL CAMINO

♦ ONE ♦

It's been more than 800 years since the time of Christ and his disciples but, as you know better than anyone, stories can leap through time and mold the reality of the present day. You have been hired by church officials in Galicia to tell stories of sacred wonders to audiences near and far.

Even you yourself don't know how much of what you've been told is true and how much has been patched together from scanty evidence and wishful thinking. You've heard of the hermit, Pelayo, who saw a shining light from heaven illuminating a humble grave in a field. When Pelayo reported his vision to the bishop, Teodomiro of Iria Flavia, the bishop had the bones exhumed, discovered a skeleton with skull detached and determined that these must be the bones of St. James who, soon after Christ's death, brought the teachings of his cousin Jesus to Spain and later was beheaded in Jerusalem. Your suspicion is that the bones may not be those of the apostle James, but you recognize the church's need for sacred relics to inspire Christian soldiers in their fight to retake Spanish territory from the Moors.

You know that repeated motifs from ancient stories resonate in the hearts of listeners and make the tales easy to believe. So, the guiding star is good material. You're thinking you'll call Pelayo a shepherd rather than a hermit.

You love the story about St. James killing Moors in battle. The vision comes right out of Revelations. When your priest starts telling that story in church, it raises the hair on your arms. As a teller of tales, you wish to have that effect on your listeners, so you will fill your version of this St. James story with the gruesome details of war. You'll describe a crucial battle; you'll call it the Battle of Clovijo. Your story will help history flow in favor of Christian Spain.

King Alfonso II had a church built over Santiago's grave in the year of our Lord 829, but you haven't seen it. You've heard it is attracting pilgrims, people who've heard the whispers about a saint who performs miracles. Your job, the church officials have made clear, is to attract more pilgrims. Your stories will attract more souls to be saved and, you can't help thinking, more money in church coffers.

In your experience, concrete symbols help people connect to less-than-concrete stories. It's like providing evidence or proof. You'll need something to show them, something your listeners can touch. A scallop shell has long been the symbol of pilgrimage. Maybe it's the lines on the shell that converge in one spot that remind people of trails from many directions leading to a sacred site. Rome and Jerusalem have been the main destinations for pilgrims so far. If you do your job well, Santiago de Campus Stellae, St. James of the Field of Stars, will become the next great focal point of religious devotion.

So yes, you'll carry a scallop shell. You'll show the paths on its surface leading to western Spain. You'll tell a story that specifically connects the shell to St. James. You have a war story, so this one should be a *romance.*

Ah, you'll tell of a bridegroom riding along the Atlantic shore toward his wedding. At that moment, the ship carrying St. James's body to Spain approaches the coastline. The groom's horse is spooked and plunges into the sea, sending its rider to a watery grave. The bride appeals to the spirit of St. James who miraculously delivers the young man back to the sand and into the arms of his loving bride-to-be. His wedding garments are covered in scallop shells.

There is a unique shiver that runs through your body when you get a story right. It's not related to cold or fear. You call it the tremor of truth, and you consider it a sign from God. It validates your calling as a storyteller. It lets you speak surely and forthrightly before audiences, your eyes glowing with the power of conviction.

♦ TWO ♦

The pope, your Holy Father, Calixtus II, believes fervently in the value of pilgrimage for the expiation of sin. You find it curious, perhaps, that he does not advocate pilgrimage to Rome where he resides but rather to Santiago de Compostela in Spain. You hold him in the highest regard as divine leader of the one true church, but you sense His Holiness does not like the smell of dirty pilgrims.

His tactics for promoting the Camino de Santiago you find brilliant. First of all, he declared any year in which St. James's day, July 25, falls on a Sunday to be a Compostelan Holy Year. The first one was in 1122, and there were almost 1000 pilgrims a day entering the city of Santiago in the weeks leading up to that sacred occasion.

Now he has commissioned you to write a guide for pilgrims on the trail. It will be known as the Codex Calixtinus. You, a simple French monk, are deeply honored that your God-given gift as a wordsmith has been recognized and placed into the service of the church by the Holy Father himself.

To prepare and research, you undertook the pilgrimage yourself in 1130 and vowed you would have the five planned volumes of the codex ready within ten years. You wrote detailed notes all along the way. As you've laid them out, the first four volumes will report the legends and miracles associated with the trail. There will be descriptions of sacred relics, shrines and churches which the devout pilgrim should visit. Also included will be relevant liturgical texts. The fifth volume will be a book of practical advice for the traveler. You want to warn pilgrims about unscrupulous and evil characters with whom they might cross paths in the roles of tax collector, innkeeper and trader. You intend also to make note of the presence of the Knights Templar who are there to protect those making their way toward Santiago. You must emphasize the importance of seeking out clean water. You'll relate the cautionary tale of a group of twenty-five travelers of whom twenty-three perished because they drank water from contaminated rivers. You'll also describe routes, accommodations, regions and peoples including those ungodly Basques and the Navarrans who disgusted you with their eating habits and speech.

You won't write of your personal pilgrimage of course, but it is that which occupies your dreams. You moved, in those months, in the company of other churchmen for whom pilgrimage is an essential aspect of a life given to God. You were gratified, as well, by the numbers of devout laymen seeking salvation.

The criminal element gave you pause. There were prisoners, walking in the presence of guards, who chose to make the difficult pilgrimage to

Santiago rather than spend several years in jail. Either pilgrimage or jail is potentially life-threatening, and the accused wretches may have opted for one punishment over the other based solely upon their physical condition at the time of sentencing. Whatever the case, you have hope for their souls.

On the other hand, there were some who pretended to travel the way in good faith but whose intentions were most sinful. You had to watch your own back and your few possessions. You prayed for these unfortunates as well, but couldn't help but think of them as being on the pathway to hell.

Walking the road to Santiago was, for you, like being on the pathway to heaven. You gloried in the air and sunshine, in the break from monastery routines, in the opportunities to meet God over and over again, around every bend in the trail. What started out as a journey of learning and cataloguing and reporting became, in addition, a journey of awakening and saying "Alleluia Amen" for the many blessings you received. You continue to receive blessings as you write the Codex Calixtinus, because putting quill to parchment requires walking again, in your memory, the Camino de Santiago.

♦ THREE ♦

You are a huge James Michener fan. Hawaii was the first truly fat book you ever read, and although you told your high school English teacher you were reading it, you didn't tell any of the kids and didn't open it where any of them could see you, because they'd have made jokes about you being a brainiac.

Later, you read The Source, and when Michener's new book Iberia came out you snapped it up even though it was non-fiction rather than eon-spanning fiction like his others.

By this time you were just about to graduate from seminary where you'd never had to hide your intellectualism. You shared some highlights of Michener's book with friends, and a couple of them asked if they could borrow it when you were done. You didn't say anything as you handed it over, but you hoped that after reading it, at least one of them would say, "Let's hike the camino." Michener devoted his final chapter to the pilgrimage trail, and it had set your imagination on fire.

One of your friends said just what you hoped. You whooped and did a little dance. You so very much wanted to follow in Michener's footsteps and to expand your spiritual horizons, but you didn't want to do it alone. Spain made you nervous. There had been so much political turmoil in the 20th century so far – a horrible civil war, acts of terrorism by ETA (the Basque nationalists) and a dictator, Franco, who was personally responsible for human rights violations in his own country as well as a severe chill in relations with other European nations.

But Franco, now, has opened the doors to tourism, and you read that last year, in 1970, over twenty million visitors from North America and Western Europe went there for vacation. But what about the pilgrimage route? Franco claimed that St. James was on his side in the Spanish Civil War, but did those boastful words make it any easier for the faithful to walk across his country? You are determined to go and make the best of it, whatever the situation might prove to be.

You research for this trip more than you researched for some of your religious studies papers. You've found out that this year, 1971, St. James Day will fall on a Sunday, and that means there should be serious celebrating going on in Santiago on July 25 if the Compostelan Holy years still matter to anyone in this day and age. You and your friend plan the trip carefully to be sure that you'll get there in time to find out for yourselves.

When the two of you arrive in Spain, you attach scallop shells to the outside of your backpacks to identify yourselves as pilgrims to anyone who might be suspicious of strangers walking their streets. And locals do look at you with surprise. Sometimes they tell you how long it's been since they last saw a pilgrim pass through – a number of days or weeks usually, but one woman claimed you two were the first pilgrims she'd seen since last year. You've been given, over garden fences, fresh tomatoes and handfuls of beans. You've been offered fresh bread and slices of yellow cake studded with dried fruit and nuts.

At the refugios, you always leave a small donation. You imagine pilgrims during the Middle Ages stopping to sleep in the same church facilities where you sleep now. You are amazed that they've remained open over the centuries even when war, disease, danger of robbery, and religious persecution kept all but a brave few away.

When you and your friend reach Santiago on July 24, you've both lost at least twenty pounds. You've tightened your belt as far as it will go and still the waistband is loose over your hip bones. After leaving your packs at the monastery hostal, the two of you enter the front gates of the cathedral. You are delighted to see how many others have come here to celebrate the Day of St. James, and as you walk around the nave, you hear a collective whisper of awe. You see visitors pointing out details of the gold and silver altar, praying before the crypt of St. James, looking along the Pórtico de la Gloria for the enchanted smile on the face of the prophet Daniel as he supposedly admires the breasts of a carved beauty opposite him. You know that later you'll see the swinging of the Botafumeiro during the pilgrim Mass and then there will be fireworks in the plaza after dark. Michener wrote about these things in his book.

But two small and quiet rituals are foremost in your mind just now. First, you wait your turn to place your hand at the base of the central column where millions of others have placed their hands before you. Your palm and fingers rest in the smooth worn recess, and you look up at the image of St. James higher on the pillar. You get the sudden and distinct feeling that he has been watching over you since the day you decided to walk the camino.

Then you approach the base of the steps behind the altar. This is a pilgrimage tradition, but that's not why you are doing it. You climb the stairs and put your arms around the statue of St. James. And this closeness to the saint who inspired your journey, this moment with your cheek against his gold cloak and your eyes closed, is the very moment when you fall softly into the arms of God.

♦ ♦ ♦

I thought I would feel history under my feet as I walked the camino, thought I would sense the ghosts of former travelers. That didn't happen. But maybe there was a bit of camino history I apprehended without knowing it at the time.

I noticed, all across Spain, a slight haziness in the air. I wondered if it was local smog (although I didn't see much in the way of spewing industry,) pollution blown in from elsewhere (at home I've seen occasional brown skies to the west indicating smog or desert sand blown from Asia,) or just the haze of humidity. Then, looking over materials about the camino after returning home, I saw an explanation I liked better.

There are lots of associations between the historical camino and the Milky Way. The camino is said to mirror, on Earth, the east/west path of the galaxy across the sky. Now, here's the good part. According to medieval legend, the Milky Way was formed from dust raised by the feet of travelling pilgrims. AHA! I thought. Obviously, some of that dust didn't rise high enough to form stars but remained in the atmosphere over Spain. Hence, the present day hazy sky.

Another explanation for the Milky Way's presence over the Camino de Santiago is that each star is the soul of a pilgrim who has died. So, I could have communed with ghosts of pilgrims past if I could have kept my eyes open late enough each evening. My difficulty staying awake to see the stars was due to Spain being the westernmost country in the Central European time zone. In May, when my husband and I were hiking, it didn't start to get light in the morning until at least 6:30 AM but stayed light in the evening until after 10:00. I was usually fast asleep by 8:30 or 9:00 each night and so didn't star gaze, or should I say "soul gaze," during the entire month we were on the trail.

Although I got no inklings of past history while walking, I definitely got a sense of history-in-the-making. During the Middle Ages, called the heyday of pilgrimages, up to 1,000 people a day arrived at the tomb of St. James. In 2010, the latest Compostelan Holy Year, 270,000 arrived in Santiago de Compostela, and that's getting pretty close to the 1,000 per day average. We can look back on the Middle Ages and come up with explanations for the popularity of pilgrimage at that time – the influence of the church, personal concern about salvation, the striving for prestige, public demonstration of gratitude, hope for healing, the need to do penance. But what will historians say about the current popularity of the camino? Something about the Age of Aquarius? The fear of apocalypse? A need to reconnect with spirit or with the land? A compulsion to try to do everything on the kick-the-bucket list?

When I asked other peregrinos what had motivated them to do the camino, everyone said a variation of the same thing – that they heard about it and knew they had to do it. As a few put it, they felt "called" to it. It seems to me that something big is doing that calling, is tapping people on the shoulder and saying, "Hey, this is for you."

Maybe that's what history-in-the-making feels like. I bet explorers like Marco Polo, Vasco da Gama and Robert Perry felt this way; scientists like Newton and Darwin and Einstein experienced it; and those seeking freedom from persecution by journeying to the New World, goldminers who went to the Klondike, and civil rights marchers in the 60s carried it in their hearts.

I am honored to have felt it, too. It feels exciting and important to be part of something bigger than myself, to be caught up in events that everyone is talking about, things that historians will create explanations for some day.

THE HEALTH CARE CAMINO

♦ ONE ♦

You walk into Pamplona on the third day of your camino. You started the hike in St. Jean Pied-de-Port, and you had done your math. You knew how many kilometers you needed to cover each day and how many days off you could take in order to reach Santiago de Compostela in time for your return flight home.

On the first day of steep uphill climbing over the Pyrenees, you met two interesting people from your home country, Ireland. Your conversations were so lively and you were having so much fun that you ignored the signals your body was sending. "Slow down," it said with greater urgency as the hours passed. "Please stop here for the day," it said in Roncesvalles, but your companions wanted to go a few kilometers farther to Auritz. You downplayed your discomfort and kept going even though you'd already done enough distance for the day to satisfy your travel plan.

On the second day, the backs of your heels and several toes on each foot had peeling, oozing red blisters, and your knees were killing you. The jabs of pain at the base of your neck from carrying a backpack were no picnic either. But still you kept up.

Your friends walked ahead this morning when you said you needed to slow your pace, and you all agreed to meet in Pamplona. You hobble into the city in the late afternoon and notice that on each street and plaza there are green and white farmacia signs. You peek into a few of these drugstores. You're used to super-mega-drug-marts that carry everything from vitamins to hair clips to eye drops to adult diapers. These businesses are about half the size of your bedroom. But front and center in each one are display racks filled with remedies for legs and feet.

You enter and feel ignorant and confused. Much of the packaging is plain and not revealing of the product within, and the labels, of course, are in Spanish. But the woman who comes forward after you say "Hola" with a pained expression on your face, is knowledgeable and helpful, and you realize she's seen it all when it comes to peregrino aches and pains.

You leave the farmacia with a bag of remedies in your hand and an elastic brace on each knee. At the albergue, there are signs on the wall about not popping blisters, applying ointment, or doing other potentially yucky things to your feet while they are up on the bed. As you sit on the edge of the lower bunk, trying not to get your hair tangled in the springs on the underside of the top bunk, you figure there must be an art to doctoring one's own feet that will take you some days to master, for sure.

The days off you had figured into your travel schedule were, you thought, for the purpose of being a tourist – going to museums,

19

walking through gardens, and admiring old buildings. But even with only three days of camino experience under your belt, you know now that the days off are going to be primarily for recuperation.

You catch up with your hiking buddies over dinner and they are disappointed when you say you can't walk with them tomorrow. You tell them your feet and legs will get better fast and that maybe you'll catch up to them by Logroño. That "maybe" is so enormous that it's blocking your vision of a rosy future reunion, but you try not to let on.

♦ TWO ♦

You were feeling so good at the beginning of your camino that you had come to the conclusion you would be spared the battles you've seen others fighting against blisters, joint problems, and sore muscles. Considering yourself lucky and maybe just slightly superhuman, you breezed right through Pamplona, Estella, and Logroño, not giving the farmacias a second glance.

But in the past few days, as you've approached Burgos, you've started wondering if you're falling apart. Your boots feel like they're two sizes too small. You'll buy a new pair while you're here in the city, but meanwhile it looks like you might lose at least one toenail. You're worried about the prospect of breaking in new boots while you're on the trail, so you might also have to buy a pair of sturdy sandals or clogs that could, if need be, support your feet while hiking without rubbing on sensitive areas. Your flimsy rubber flip-flops definitely cannot serve as back-up.

The ankle that you badly sprained three years ago isn't exactly hurting, but it doesn't feel reliable on the rocky uphills and downhills or on uneven paving stones. Worst of all is the increasingly sharp pain along the front of your lower leg. Shin splints are not good news for someone who just wants to get up tomorrow morning and walk, who gets stir-crazy at the thought of taking a day off.

You met a mother-daughter team yesterday and not only did the daughter have one calf wrapped to ease her shin-splint pain, but the two of them had hiked, only a little more slowly than usual, through two days of vomiting and diarrhea. Part of you thinks, if they can do it so can you. The other part of you considers the fact that Burgos is a transportation hub in this part of Spain, and if you're going to have to call it quits, this might be a smart time to do it.

♦ THREE ♦

You just learned about the Camino de Santiago a month before you started in Sarria. You had a week's vacation coming up and you read on Wikipedia that if you hiked at least the final 100 kilometers into Santiago de Compostela, you would receive a pilgrim certificate at the end. What a lark, you thought.

You've never hiked before, so you bought boots. They felt pretty comfortable in the shoe store. You borrowed a backpack and raingear then followed advice that you read on websites about packing light. You don't own any wool socks, but you figured your cotton and synthetic ones would be fine for five or six days. You put some tiger balm and band-aids in your first aid kit.

You made your way via plane and bus to Sarria at kilometer 113. You picked up your pilgrim passport at the albergue, got your first stamp in it, and set out early next morning. When you passed the

100 kilometer stone marker three hours later, you were in high spirits. The Galician countryside is magical, and after one long uphill at the start of the day, you felt like you were walking through postcard heaven – scenic view after scenic view of rustic villages, rolling fields, and pastures enclosed by curved stone walls.

You've always been fit, so you are surprised, after a lunch break at a bar/café, by how stiff and gimpy you feel. You sit back down and stretch the tight places in your back and legs then take off your boots and socks and cover the sensitive places on your feet with band-aids. You think about the stand that was set up just past the 100 kilometer marker where someone was selling walking sticks, scallop shells and calabashes. At the time, you'd chuckled inwardly, thinking that stuff was just for people who wanted the pilgrim look.

In the next hour, you find out that band-aids are worthless for preventing blisters. You stop in a farmacia for something better. What do they call these things? Sticking plasters? Moleskin? How can you communicate what you need in sign language? While you're there, you get some sunscreen, because you can feel your face and lips starting to fry. Then, luckily, you find a place just around the corner from the farmacia that sells walking sticks. You hold a few in your hand to test the heft and height. You leave the shop some euros lighter, leaning on the companion that you will credit with the miracle of getting your aching body into Santiago by the end of the week.

♦ ♦ ♦

It looked to me as though the ladies from Austria who ran the albergue in Los Arcos really understood the health care needs of peregrinos. They had a small blue trough on the back patio with a bench alongside so you could sit and soak your feet in salt water. They served wonderful brown bread for breakfast. They also had a sign-up sheet at the reception desk for twenty minute massages. I put my name down.

After a shower and a change into Capri length pants, I went to the corner of the dining area that was sectioned off with sheets hung on a line. The masseur asked in Spanish and sign language if it was my back giving me trouble, and I said, "No, it's my legs," and pointed down at them. His eyes widened and he called over a woman to translate. After he spoke, she said, "You have really red stripes on your legs, and he's afraid the massage will hurt you." I assured them that there was no pain, itchiness or discomfort. It was just my skin's strange and ugly reaction to Mediterranean heat and sun.

He proceeded to work, knead, cajole and partially convince some of the knots and taut ropes in my legs to relax. He advised, again in Spanish and mime, that I tighten the waist strap of my backpack higher on my body, above my hip bones, so that it wouldn't compress the top of the ilio-tibial band which runs down the side of the thigh and connects at the back of the knee. Bingo! I knew he'd accurately diagnosed part of my leg problem.

When I emerged from the massage area, an English-speaking woman, who'd overheard everything while sitting on the other side of the dining room writing in her journal, said, "Can I see what's up with your legs?"

So I slightly raised the hem of my pants and turned each leg this way and that. "Yikes!" she said.

"It started out as a heat rash under the tops of my socks," I said, "and then I scrunched the socks down and maybe got a nasty sun poisoning on top of the rash." Also, I'd been wrapping my knees every morning since before Pamplona, and maybe the restricted circulation had something to do with it. Anyway, it was frightful. Little bent-over Spanish women on their way to evening Mass the past few days had stared at my legs as if worried I was bringing disease into their villages.

The woman, from Toronto, had tea tree oil in her first aid kit and suggested I try it since it had helped a rash she'd had a few days prior. I only put it on that once, but the redness faded over the next few days and, thank goodness, never reappeared.

We sat together over dinner that evening and talked some more. She said, "The camino's really good at finding your weak places and making you pay attention to them." We both had examples of injuries that had happened to us ten, twenty, thirty years ago that were making nuisances of themselves as we hiked day after day, with weight on our backs, on some pretty unforgiving surfaces.

I recalled the time when I was about thirty when I giddily rushed down a mountainside, hit level ground with a thud, fell, and wrenched a knee, my right knee, the same knee that was bugging me now as I hiked. I remembered being fourteen and trying out for cheerleading. I did a cartwheel into a forward split and ripped a groin muscle (right side again!) so badly that it took two years to heal. And then there was the long-distance bicycle trip I did about twenty years ago. The balls of my feet pushed those pedals for over a thousand miles, and then one evening in the shower, I washed between my toes and felt acute pain in the middle of my foot. A bursa had popped between the metatarsals, and I was on crutches for three days. So the twinges I was feeling in my feet while hiking were making me very nervous.

I proceeded to develop a personal health care regimen over my weeks on the camino, and it got me through. At the end of each day's walking, I took aspirin to reduce the swelling in my knees then lay on the bed or floor to do at least a half hour of stretches and foot massage. In the shower, I did hot and cold spray treatments from the knees down and was very gentle about washing between my toes. In the mornings, I took Vitamin C for anti-inflammatory benefits, calcium-magnesium to prevent muscle cramping, iron to help my blood absorb oxygen, and zinc for its moderating effect on sweat and body odor (not a problem for me before this hike, but all the exertion must have started cleaning out deep layers of toxins.) For breakfast I drank tea instead of coffee because it's easier on my joints, and throughout the day I drank a lemony electrolyte drink that was available everywhere, including in the official, bright red Camino de Santiago beverage machines!

I also considered my walking style. After one long afternoon of hiking into Belorado on the left-sloped side of a dirt road, I realized that I was rolling inward on the arch of my right foot as it gave in to gravity. I tried thereafter to find a level surface to walk on, or I switched back and forth from right to left, probably making my husband feel like he was in a day-long do-si-do. Two weeks later, in the process of struggling down the long hill into Triacastela, I watched a Pakistani man who had the most wonderful relaxed, slightly springy, and smooth gait. I tried to walk like he did, and it helped. I had been reacting to knee pain by tightening up – not a good idea.

There were times, in self-pity mode, when I thought I was the only one having so much physical trouble. I didn't see other people doing stretches or taking vitamins or leaning heavily on their trekking poles on the downhills. Then one day, I saw two men whose knees were so stiff that they couldn't reach their own feet to bandage them. They had to sit opposite each other on a bench to apply medicine and adhesive to each other's feet. As the weather warmed up, and short pants replaced long, I noticed quite a number of wrapped knees and ankles as well as a few scarlet-red rashes. I came upon more peregrinos taking long breaks, removing their shoes and socks, lying on the ground and stretching their legs upward along the trunks of trees. I met a woman, late one hot afternoon, whose face was bright red except for her lips which were smeared with white zinc oxide. She looked desperate as she asked where the albergue was and unhappy as I pointed up the long and steep set of stairs that led to the old city at the top of the hill.

It truly amazes me that one can walk long hours on the camino and not hear moans and groans and sighs and gasps of pain. But each day, each hour, each passing of familiar and unfamiliar faces is the same -- "Hola. Buen Camino," said in a cheerful tone. Sometimes it's "Buenos Dias." "Bonjour." "Guten Tag." "Hello." And every once in a while, all of the greetings are joined together and spoken fast like a run-on sentence. Then there's laughter all around, and, as they say, that's the best medicine of all.

MUSICAL CAMINO

♦ ONE ♦

As you walk up the long valley toward Galicia, you take a break to look ahead in your guidebook. You want to see what's in store for you over the next week or so until you reach Santiago. You read that, in Triacastela, you'll have to make a choice to either take the northern route through small villages and rural countryside or the southern route, which involves more roadside walking but takes you via Samos, home of one of the oldest monasteries in the western world. The guidebook recommends an overnight stop there to hear "Gregorian songs" sung during the evening Mass in the monastery church. You love the mystical sound of Gregorian chants. You keep a CD of them in your car to keep your blood pressure in check during rush hour traffic jams. Now, you'll get to hear it live!

The day you walk to Samos is drizzly and foggy. The monastery, seen from a bluff above town as you approach, looks like a fortress, square and heavy with dark angled roofs. You wind your way steeply down the trail to the main street of town which is bordered by old-fashioned lampposts and wrought-iron fences with a scallop shell design. The curving metal shapes are reflected on wet sidewalks.

You spend the chilly afternoon getting groceries, drinking hot tea with a shot of rum, and doing laundry. You lean against the warm dryer as it tumbles your clothes. You tuck yourself into a corner away from the drafty door of a restaurant to eat a leisurely dinner until it's time to go to the 7:30 Mass.

You're wearing your wool long-john shirt, a sweatshirt and your rain jacket, because you have a feeling it will be cold in the church. Sure enough, of the twenty-five or so people attending the service, no one has taken off any layers.

Seven monks in white robes, two in black, and two men in street clothes file onto the dais in front of the altar, and the service begins. But the music is not at all what you expected. An elderly and creaky-voiced abbot sings a line, and the others sing back to him. This is liturgical singing as you've heard it in so many other churches, although here there is more of it. Sometimes a round-faced monk sings solo for a while. He definitely has the most pleasing voice of the group.

You feel your blood-pressure rising. Either the guidebook was wrong or there's a big hole in your understanding of what Gregorian music actually is.

When you're stuck in traffic at home, the music distracts you from the upsetting visual of guardrail-to-guardrail exhaust-spewing cars ahead of you. Now you find yourself looking around the church to find a visual to distract you from this disappointing music.

First you study the tall altar, which is amazingly modern considering the age of this monastery. You think there was something in the guidebook about a fire. Was it a distillery fire? You imagine the monks stepping on grapes and stirring big vats.

Then you check out the long table at the front of the dais that holds the communion dishes. There are two large heads carved and painted into the panel under the tabletop. At first, you assume it is Jesus and Mary, but then you notice they are wearing crowns and might be a king and queen. The female is blond and reminds you of Jeannie on "I Dream of Jeannie."

You look more closely at the two statues of soldiers to the right and left of the front pew. Each has his sword raised and has one foot resting on a decapitated head. Yuck, you think.

Suddenly, white-robed, black-robed and plain-clothes singers leave the dais leaving only the round-faced soloist. He comes to the podium and speaks to the assembled peregrinos for the first time. His voice comforts you. Then he closes his eyes, puts his hands together and sings once more. When he picks up the silver chalice and walks among the congregation sprinkling holy water, the blessed droplets striking everyone's plastic or nylon or Gore-tex rain jackets make a sweet sort of music.

♦ TWO ♦

Your grandfather always told you not to waste a good yawn. All that lung power should carry a tune while it's at it. He could yawn phrases of church hymns and beginning notes of symphonies. You usually just sing five descending notes during your yawns.

You thought about this potential use of lung power as you hiked the steep trail out of St. Jean Pied-de-Port and over the Pyrenees Mountains. You were huffing and puffing. You hadn't realized how cardio-vascular this was going to be. There was no way you'd have any breath to spare for a tune.

But as you trudged, the Volga Boatman's Song came to mind. You started singing it, and somehow those deep resonant notes pulled you up the hill, like the Russian boatmen of centuries past pulled barges up the Volga River.

Your aerobic fitness level increased rapidly over the next few days of traversing foothills, and you got into the habit of singing your way uphill. "Climb Ev'ry Mountain" was a good one, and you had fun with that Fal-de-ri song from your childhood that starts out, "I love to go a-wandering along a mountain path." On a moan-and-groan kind of day, you substituted the word "pilgrim" for "hound-dog" on the chorus of the Elvis song. On a good day, it was "Zip-a-dee-doo-dah."

When you ran out of song ideas, you whistled Sousa marches, but you only knew a few. The hills were running out as you neared Burgos, and so was your musical repertoire.

Then you found the harmonica. It was on the windowsill above the upper bunk where you slept in Hornillos del Camino. Someone's really going to miss this, you figured. But what would be the likelihood of your catching up to someone who was at least a day ahead of you on the trail. And what would you do -- walk up to everyone you saw to ask them if they'd lost a harmonica? No, the best way to put the word out was to play it.

Except you didn't know how to play a harmonica. But the cool thing you discovered about this instrument was that you could make pleasing sounds just by goofing around with it.

So that's how you crossed the meseta. The breathing was easy and steady, and you played the harmonica and taught yourself as you walked. No one turned around and said, "Hey, that's my harmonica," and a good thing too, because you'd started thinking of it as yours. You even have the perfect little pocket for it in your vest.

Now, on the final day of your walk to Santiago, there are more hills than you thought there would be. It's quite a morning of climbing up to Monte do Gozo, but the guidebook said nothing about this in the flurry of details about getting to the destination. You need a tune to get you up the steep parts. So you pull out the harmonica and start playing "Climb Ev'ry Mountain" without any forethought, without questioning whether you could play it or not.

And an hour later, when you stand on Monte do Gozo by the huge monument commemorating papal visits, the song is still going through your head, as songs tend to do. You look out over the rooftops of Santiago and hear, with full orchestral back-up, "Til you find your dream." Indeed.

♦ THREE ♦

You used to listen to rock-and-roll through earphones. All the kids at your high school did. You loved the way the music filled you up, blocked out the rest of the world and made you want to dance. But that was before you started your training as a psychiatric nurse and learned that some schizophrenic patients wear headphones to diminish the disturbing voices in their heads. The voices told one male patient to kill you, and he almost did before other staff could restrain him.

You don't work at that hospital now, and you certainly don't wear headphones any more. You were on disability for two years because you were afraid to leave the house.

You are walking the camino with your best friend as part of your ongoing therapy. You can't help noticing, with a start, the peregrinos with wires dangling from their ears. Some are young people listening to music, like you once did. But there are others who, you can tell, are troubled souls. They look down a lot and can't meet people's eyes. They walk with an awkward heaviness. They sit alone and fiddle with their things. They talk in non sequiturs.

Your friend has good radar. She can tell when you're getting agitated. She'll move toward you on the trail to let people pass by on her side. She lets you sit in the restaurant seat with its back to the wall. She takes care of booking ahead for every night's accommodation so the two of you can have a private room with bath. She steers conversations onto easy topics.

Camino therapy is working, you can tell. Your fight-or-flight responses have mellowed during the three and a half weeks you've been walking, even in the vicinity of peregrinos you've informally diagnosed as crazy persons. The atmosphere of friendliness and helpfulness and trust on the camino is good medicine. Where else in the world have you ever felt so safe?

It's easier to keep your breathing steady these days, and you don't feel compelled, every thirty seconds, to turn around to see who's behind you. Your friend squeezed your arm yesterday and said, "You're doing so well."

You're trying to stay in the moment and not worry about the future. But two questions occur to you. Will you be able to hold onto this calmer state when you reach Santiago, the biggest city since León (where you had a few moments of near-panic)? And will you find yourself permanently improved when your camino is over and you return home?

You and your friend walk into Santiago on a Sunday morning. Suddenly you are surrounded by the sounds of church bells. They come from all directions, and the two of you try to spot each bell tower over rooftops, but it's impossible. The sound fills you up and carries you, and you remember, as a teenager, being carried away and dancing to music, when joy was inside you and life was innocent.

You've asked yourself if learning, the hard way, that the world is not a very safe place means that trust has to go. The camino has given you the answer already. Opposites co-exist. It's like the yin-yang symbol – the dark and light wrap around each other, rock and roll with each other.

And this is how you come back home to yourself. You spend your day and a half in Santiago not shopping or sightseeing or drinking coffee or wine with fellow peregrinos. You find a place to sit and listen to one street musician, then another, and another. You enjoy the Gypsy guitarist, the South American salsa band, the hammer dulcimer player, the bagpiper, the harpist, and the trio of accordion and balalaika players. You close your eyes. You find the joy inside.

◆ ◆ ◆

It was a misty morning when my husband and I began the uphill trek out of Rabanal towards the Cruz de Ferro. It was frustrating knowing there were beautiful views out there, somewhere, and not being able to see more than twenty meters in any direction.

I started listening instead of looking. I physically separated myself from conversations ahead of and behind me and got cozy with the hush. I listened to the polyrhythms of breathing, footsteps and walking sticks. I noticed different qualities of crunch underfoot.

Time flew, and next thing I knew the crumbling walls of Foncebadón appeared out of the fog, and a craving for a second cup of tea grabbed me. Older guidebooks call this place an abandoned village. But rocks from fallen buildings have been moved, positioned and cemented to form new albergues, stores and bars. The town is a phoenix rising from the ashes.

And then I heard the phoenix song. A café had speakers placed under its eaves and classical music was playing. I started to hum along.

"What is that music?" I asked my husband. He could hum it too, but neither of us could name it even as we continued racking our brains while sipping our hot drinks and eating croissants. We found the music a very welcome change from the Spanish MTV that's often on television in many establishments.

The fog was still thick as we continued walking up the mountain. We wondered if it was possible to miss seeing the Cruz de Ferro because of low visibility.

Then all of a sudden, there it was, right in front of us, right beside the path, right beside a road. From photos I'd seen of it, I thought it was way up on top of a bare pinnacle. Nope. It stood on its own dirt and rock mound, but there were trees and other hills to all sides.

Here's what was lovely. A young man stood praying on the mound, his head bowed, his hands on the wood post supporting the iron cross. To the right were two peregrinos, leaning against the fence, whispering quietly. To the left was a bicyclist at the edge of the road, pausing to catch his breath and to appreciate his accomplishment before the long descent to come. My husband and I stood at the foot of this human cross and didn't, or couldn't, move until the praying man was finished. It seemed as though we were antennae helping to channel his prayers.

A minute later, when we had walked only about fifty steps further along the camino, an unearthly and beautiful song reached us from the direction of the cross behind us, hidden again in the fog. We tried to think of who was following us on the trail. Which woman in the coffee shop in Foncebadón could have been a singing angel in disguise?

Just then, the mist lifted as though carried away by her voice, and we saw blue sky and green mountains topped with purple heather to the west. We walked toward beauty, and the song accompanied us all the way to the sun.

THE FOOD AND WINE CAMINO

♦ ONE ♦

It's your first evening in Spain, and you don't know how the food thing works here. You ask, in your limited Spanish, about dinner at the restaurant in your hotel, and they say dinner's at eight. But it's only 5:30 and you're starving after having hiked for five hours today.

You see a few peregrinos sitting outside a small bar having a glass of wine. You shyly approach the counter and try asking again. "¿La cena? Dinner?"

The owner draws you a picture. There's an oval — that's a platter. "¿Pescado?" he asks. When you nod yes, he draws a fish at one end of the oval. "¿Ensalata?" he continues, and you nod even bigger, because after having eaten plane and train food for the past twenty-four hours, you'd love a fresh salad. Then he draws something else on the plate which you agree to even though you have no idea what it is. "Y vino tinto, red wine, por favor," you add.

Your meal comes, and there are five small whole fish, fried to a golden crispiness, the typical ensalata mixta of this part of Spain consisting of lettuce, mild white onions, carrots, tomatoes, white asparagus, green olives and tuna. And the surprise item is a small portion of fries, but not like the processed kind you're used to from North America. These are cut strips of just-peeled potatoes, cooked in the lightest oil you can imagine, and with a touch of salt. You would never dream of dousing these with ketchup even if such a thing were on the table.

After two small glasses of wine, you are feeling content and satisfied. You get the bill and, at first, think it must be wrong. Such a low total! Then you see that each glass of wine cost only sixty cents. And the food, fresh and local, with no shipping and processing costs attached, is the kind of bargain that budget travelers dream of.

♦ TWO ♦

You've just graduated from university in Germany and only learned of the camino two weeks before hopping on the train to your starting point for the hike. Now you don't know what possessed you. You still live at your parents' house, and you like your mother's cooking. You've traveled a bit in Europe – a few days here, a week there – but always in the company of family or friends. Here you are alone, in a country where you don't know one word of the language, and the food looks very strange to you. You remember when you were little and having a meal out somewhere. You were encouraged to try one bite of everything. More than you like to admit to yourself, you ended up sneaking half-chewed bits into your napkin.

The albergues usually have snack machines, so you often buy a package of cookies and a juice or a pop for breakfast. Every day, you buy a bocadillo for lunch, because it's just a baguette with meat or cheese on it, and you know there won't be any weird surprises. At the end of a day of hiking, the young people staying at an albergue often chip in together and buy groceries to cook a dinner. You're getting pretty tired of spaghetti.

One evening in Burgos, you go to a tapas bar at the invitation of an older couple you walked with that day. All along the bar there is an amazing spread of attractive food, but except for potato salad, olives, and some marinated mushrooms, you can't identify anything. The folks you're with know a little Spanish, so they help you choose a few dishes. After just a few bites, you're delighted by how much you like this food. The flavors zing your taste buds more than your mother's cooking ever has.

The couple has ordered a few mystery items, and the man is chewing away at little tubular fried bits, unable to come up with a guess as to what he's eating. "Not much flavor," he says. "And the texture is kind of like fat, but not exactly." He offers you one, and you decline. As you leave the tapas bar together and walk down the alleyway, you see live snails in a barrel outside a small market. The man stops, points at them and laughs. He figures that's what the tubular tapas were. You are so glad you didn't eat one.

♦ THREE ♦

In some of the places where a pilgrims' menu is served, usually for eight to ten euros including wine and dessert, there are large tables where you eat with people from any number of different countries. Everyone talks about the camino, and everyone talks about food.

In León, you remember telling your dinner companions that at first you were disappointed by the fairly small size of the portions in Spain, but you had gotten used to it and actually liked not pigging out at the end of a day. Someone at the table mentioned a study he had read about places in the world where living to be 100 is a relatively common occurrence. In Okinawa, for instance, children are taught to eat just until they are 80% full, and Okinawans attribute their good health and longevity to this practice.

Now that you're in Galicia, your new awareness and appreciation of the 80% sensation is flying out the dining room window. The portions are huge, and the food is simple and simply yummy. You were taught, as a child, to clean your plate, but even if you weren't trying to stay somewhat close to the 80% mark, you would find it impossible to eat up all that is set in front of you each evening. This is farm country, and these are farm-sized meals. The slender Spaniards you saw and met during the first 600 kilometers of your walk have given way to hefty, stocky Galicians, whose gardens and corn fields and flocks and herds you admire along every step of the way in this fertile green northwestern corner of Spain.

◆ ◆ ◆

The day I arrived home after walking the Camino de Santiago, I stopped in the local liquor store to check out the Spanish wine section. I had felt unsure in that department in the past because of the unfamiliar grape varieties listed on the labels – Airen, Albariño, and Verdejo among the whites, and Tempranillo, Cencibel, and Garnacha in the reds. I didn't learn a thing about grape varieties along the camino, because the wine I so thoroughly enjoyed there came by the glass, the unmarked bottle, or in a large pitcher. Best of all, it only cost two to six euros a bottle. It was young wine, I think, and with no bottling, labeling, or shipping costs, it was cheaper than mineral water.

In one instance, it was free. There was a courtyard beside the Bodegas Irache winery just west of Estella where you could help yourself to a taste of wine from a tap at the wall. Actually there were two taps. One said "Vino" and the other said "Agua." A few peregrinos did fill their water bottles at the "Agua" tap, but the line-up was at the "Vino" tap.

I feel braver in the liquor store now, more willing to take chances, because every glass of wine I drank in Spain was wonderful. Being brave about trying new things can be tricky for North Americans. We are accustomed to a standardized food industry and a culinary culture that's spread across a huge continent. It's not just that a Big Mac in Toronto tastes the same as a Big Mac in Reno. It's that omelettes are omelettes, and tea with cream is just that, and toast is slices of bread browned and crisped up. On the other hand, if you ask for tortilla in Spain, sometimes you'll get a slice of mouthwatering potato-egg pie, and sometimes you'll get an omelette. If you order té con leche, as I do for breakfast, sometimes you'll get steamed milk in the tea, sometimes steamed milk on the side, and sometimes cold milk on the side. Tostada, or toast, the most common breakfast, although sometimes croissants or pastries are available, can mean small slices of toasted baguette or a baguette cut in half lengthwise and grilled, and rarely will it mean slices of toasted bread in the shape North Americans are used to.

Luckily, I liked either kind of tortilla, and tea prepared in any fashion. I have slight wheat allergies so on a few mornings I ate yoghurt I had purchased the previous evening at a supermercado. But otherwise, I ate tostada for breakfast, because that's all that was available.

My husband and I carried crackers, rounds of local cheese, and apples or dried fruit for snacks or lunches. Evening meals were a mixed bag, and as the journey went on, we gained more clues as to how to eat when, and what, we wanted. Pilgrim meals, offered some places, were a good deal and might be served as early as 6:00 or 6:30 if we were lucky. If the town was large enough to have a choice of eateries, we could usually find a tapas bar, a place with a sign saying "cafetería" (although not a self-serve cafeteria as seen in North American), or a place that specialized in pasta and pizza. Sometimes we just looked in the door to see if there was food on the counter or menus sitting on the tables. All of these were places with flexible serving times.

After one chilly day of walking in the rain, none of our food-searching techniques was working, and I needed to eat to warm up. In Azofra, there were only two bars, one of which served dinner at 7:00. The other had a lone plate of potato tortilla sitting on the bar. We asked for tortilla with cheese melted on top, which at least took the edge off my hunger. "¿Para beber?" asked the bartender. Ah yes, what to drink. I didn't want caffeine so late in the afternoon. The thought of beer or wine made me colder. "I know. Whiskey!" I said. The bartender made a face. Maybe Spaniards don't consider whiskey an afternoon drink, but it sure warmed my insides on that gray wet windy day.

My husband and I don't say grace before eating, although every once in a while, I'll blurt a favorite from my teenage years – "Rub-a-dub-dub, thanks for the grub. Yea God!" But during our walk to Santiago, we were very aware of, and grateful for, the gifts we received at the table. Fresh squeezed orange juice, wonderful coffee, local fruit and vegetables, pulpo (marinated octopus), Galician stew, potato tapas with garlic mayonnaise, calamari right out of the ocean, giant green olives, crusty bread, paella (a sizzling skillet of rice and seafood), beer, wine or whiskey, and interesting people from all over the world to talk with over meals.

THE ROCK CAMINO

You are sixteen, and except for a fourteen year old boy who's hiking with his father, you are the youngest person that you know of on the trail. You are walking with a teacher from the school where you were placed to get you away from an abusive home. One of your brothers beat you and left you in the snow to die. Then, your best friend committed suicide the week before you started the camino. You realize that if you weren't here walking, you'd be thinking about following her lead.

Along the trail, there are concrete markers with the scallop shell design on them that show which path to follow. There are often small rocks placed on top of the markers, and you've heard that the stones represent people's prayers. You look around for big rocks to add to the piles, because your prayers are so huge.

One afternoon in a big dorm room full of bunk beds, you start talking to a woman who has smiled at you the last few days when you've passed each other along the trail. To your surprise, you find yourself telling her about your friend's death and how you were the one who found her body hanging. She holds your hand as you cry. Then she asks you if you've picked up rocks for your friend. You shake your head and wonder why you hadn't thought of this.

The next day, as you start to walk, you picture your friend's face and let your focus go soft while your eyes sweep the trail ahead. Meanwhile, you talk to your teacher, you smile, and say "Hola" to other peregrinos, and you drink from your water bottle, all as if it were a morning like any other. Then suddenly you see the rock you were meant to find. It is so small! It is pink and orange with lines crisscrossing it like veins, and it is slightly lobed. When you hold it in the center of your palm, maybe it is touching one of your own pulse points, but you swear you can feel it beating. You put the hand holding the rock against your own heart, and you walk that way for the rest of the morning. You feel stronger with every step.

♦ TWO ♦

You skimmed some information about the camino online before you left home. There was a lot of advice about what to pack and what not to pack. You saw some notes about a tradition of bringing a rock from your home to leave by an iron cross on a hill between Rabanal and Ponferrada. One website called it an offering toward world peace; one called it a token of love; a few suggested the rock is a metaphor for a burden or sin. You don't know which of these it represents to you as you pack a rock into the bottom of your backpack. You'll figure it out as you go.

45

After three days on the trail and chafed shoulders where the straps of your backpack rub, you decide to get rid of the rock. It's stupid to carry any extra weight on the camino. Everybody knows that, and the proof is in seeing all the peregrinos heading to the post office to mail off extra clothes, journals, toiletries, cups and bowls, Spanish grammar books, bathing suits and anything else that's not essential each and every day.

You find a lovely pine tree in a peaceful spot, sit underneath for a water break and take the rock out of your pack. But you find you can't leave it there. It doesn't feel right.

The next day you lay it at the base of a statue of Jesus on the cross. No go. "What's the big deal?" you say to yourself as you repack the rock.

You feel kind of pissed off about the rock for three weeks, all the way to Rabanal then up, up, up that steady slope. You think maybe you fell for some trick, that really no one except you is dumb enough to have carried a stone all the way from home.

But then you see the iron cross up on top of a big pole, silhouetted against the sky. On the mound around it are hundreds, maybe thousands, of rocks. Some are painted – there are a bunch of pink ones that might be the rocks contributing to world peace. Many have the names of hometowns written on them. You read them as you look for the perfect spot for your rock.

A peregrino you've seen here and there for the past week walks up to the cross, digs a rock out of his pack, grins at you and shrugs as if affirming the zaniness of lugging stones. He lays it near the cross then takes off down the trail. You look at his rock. It has something written on it, but it's not a place name.

"Solvitur ambulando," it says. "It is solved by walking." And the quote is attributed to Augustine of Hippo. You put your rock right beside his to share in some of that wisdom. You feel the gift of peace, the gift of love, and the lightening of a burden as you look at the two rocks sitting side by side among so many others, and you laugh because you carried the silly sin of being pissed off for three weeks instead of figuring out for yourself what value there was in carrying a stone.

♦ THREE ♦

You graduated a few years ago in computer science. You go to work each day in light-weight clean clothes, and when you get home each evening, they look as good as they did that morning. At work you are a juggler, a juggler of things that have no weight but that have potentially huge significance. There's a power that runs through you when you're on the job that feels electrical, atomic, packed with information, and at least as fast as space travel.

You took three weeks off from your job to hike the camino. When your co-workers asked why, you didn't have a real answer. So you said, "For a change of pace."

No kidding, you realize now. Twenty-five kilometers per day compared to the speed of space travel? People at the office would laugh. They'd pity you.

When you started out from León, you had to convince yourself that, no, gravity couldn't be stronger in Spain than it was back home. So why did you feel so slow and heavy? Even your brain felt like lead.

But as your thinking slowed down to walking speed, you started to see what was around you. And what you saw was stones. Paving stones

47

on streets and sidewalks, stones stacked in layers or stood up edgewise for fences, stone houses and barns and granaries, big piles of rocks stacked by peregrinos, stone statuary, rocky paths leading up and down hills and into and out of villages, rock cliffs, rocky stream beds and, best of all, great granite cathedrals.

You try to imagine mere mortals moving and lifting huge blocks of stone, carving intricate details year after year and, in some cases, century after century. You want to walk right up to the cathedral walls and touch them where the sun has warmed them, but you also want to stand far away so that you can take it all in, all that majesty.

It is in the Praza do Obradoiro, admiring the western façade of the Catedral del Apóstol, the cathedral of the apostle James, that you discover the real significance of gravity. The feeling of heaviness that troubled you at the beginning of your hike disappeared after a few days on the trail. But now you realize it's been the stones themselves holding you, attracting you, keeping you in their energy field. They've slowed time to such a degree that your three weeks in Spain have become a lifetime of experience so condensed that it gleams like quartz.

You sit on a bench in that magnificent square in the afternoon sunshine and take off your shoes and socks. You rest your tired feet on the smooth paving stones and feel a power that's electrical, atomic, packed with information, and as slow as forever.

♦ ♦ ♦

When I was a kid, I always had a rock in my pocket. I'd choose one that was smooth and that had warm colors or cool colors, and it would give me comfort to hold it, to roll it back and forth in my hand – like rosary beads, perhaps. Although there were no words that went along with my touching of the rock, still it was like praying because it connected me to something ineffable.

When I began my camino, I was intrigued seeing people put stones on trail markers or by statues then stopping and praying. I thought I would feel self-conscious doing that. But high on the hill called Alto de Erro between Roncesvalles and Subiri, at a memorial for a peregrino who had died there, passersby had laid pine cones all over and around it, and I felt moved to add one, too.

From there, I started to string a line of prayers that would stretch all the way across Spain and beyond. Sometimes I would see a rock on the trail that reminded me of someone. Not that the person's face was suggested in the patterns on the stone or that a certain rock was so-and-so's favorite color. Nothing so clearly definable. I'd just pick up the rock, sense who it was for, and carry it to a place that felt sacred -- maybe influenced by the play of light and shadow or the view from that spot or the way plants and trees enclosed it. There I'd place the rock and give it a pat before walking on.

Sometimes I saw the sacred site first then looked around for a stone. Everywhere there were rocks, many plain ordinary ones but, without fail, always some that held special beauty or mysterious hieroglyphs.

I started the string of prayers by picking up rocks for my aunts and uncles, I don't know why. Although two of my parents' siblings have died, I laid stones for all three of my mom's brothers and their wives, and all three of my dad's sisters and their husbands. There was no rush to this process. It took several days. Then I searched the ground for four rocks that made me think of my siblings. Another rock along the way contained all four of my grandparents. One with a pink spot at one end and an orange spot at the other became my parents. It felt significant to find them joined in one rock, since I think they both would have said that their marriage was not a very happy one.

I left many rocks in beautiful places for my son who struggles with mental illness. And a stone in the shape of a crystalline arrow became a prayer for my husband's and my continued journey together.

Between Belorado and San Juan de Ortega is a long uphill climb over the Montes de Oca. At the top, there is a memorial to Spanish Republicans who were executed there by Franco's troops during the Spanish Civil War in the late 1930s. The memorial could not be built until after Franco's death in 1975. At its base, I left a rock that looked to me like a broken heart.

After receiving our pilgrim certificates in Santiago de Compostela, my husband and I walked the additional ninety kilometers to Finisterre. We dropped our packs off at a hotel, then hiked the last three kilometers to the cape, the second westernmost point in mainland Europe. I had visions of selecting one last rock and throwing a final prayer toward the setting sun and watching it splash into the Atlantic. But physical prayers have to adapt to physical realities, and the ruggedness of the coastline didn't allow me within throwing distance of the water. There was a small cross sitting like an afterthought among the boulders, almost as if it had been randomly tossed out of the squat lighthouse that warns boats away from that dangerous point of land. On one of the arms of that cross, I put a prayer for the continuation of life even as my camino was ending.

Just as my habit of picking up rocks started long before I walked the camino, so it will continue long after. A few days after I arrived home, I found a level area on which to build a stone labyrinth. I cannot even imagine how many rocks it will take. Like the camino, it's a big project that will get done one step, one rock at a time.

THE ANIMAL CAMINO

You love how walking through northern Spain in May takes you along narrow farm roads edged with red poppies, between fields of young grape vines and sunflowers. Every so often you plunge into the shade of a sheltering stand of trees, mostly pines and oaks. Birds chatter and chirp, and there's one kind of bird that you hear over and over again. At first you tell yourself it's a call you've never heard before, but then you stop in your tracks realizing you know what it is.

"Oh my gosh, it's a cuckoo!" you say out loud. You're sure you're right because, as a child, you watched Looney Tunes cartoons, and there was a demented cuckoo that burst from a clock on the end of a spring and did an insistent and insane call until someone took a hammer to it. Also, one of your childhood friends had a cuckoo clock in his house, a souvenir from Bavaria, but you only heard it once because his mother hated it and turned off the cuckoo mechanism. Now, here is that sound but coming from somewhere above you in the treetops.

A peregrino coming up behind has heard your exclamation and laughs. He's German, although not Bavarian, and he tells you that when he was a boy, he tried to sneak up on the cuckoos he heard in the woods. In all his attempts, and he was quite persistent, the closest he ever came to success was seeing the rustle of leaves as one flew away.

A similar experience of recognition occurs in Nájera when a large bird flies over the red-tiled roofs, its long white neck and head stretched forward, its black-tipped wings wide, and skinny legs dangling. The only thing missing is a pink or blue bundled baby hanging from its beak. The stork lands on top of the church tower, and then you see that not only the tower but the entire red striated cliff face behind the town is alive with the bobbing heads and waving wings of young ones in their nests waiting for their parents to return with food. Your fascination with bird-watching and bird-listening along the camino is enhanced by the strong contradiction between nature's reality and the silly kitsch about cuckoos and storks in the North American media and marketplace.

♦ TWO ♦

You're not a dog person. In fact, at home, dogs have always made you nervous, and it's a vicious cycle. They sense your fear and growl or bark at you. But dogs are everywhere along the camino, and most of them are loose. At first you did your usual dog avoidance maneuvers - - slowing your pace, lowering your gaze, murmuring "good dog, good dog," and giving them wide berth. Then you realized that all of that was totally unnecessary. Camino dogs don't even lift their heads or give a single yip as you pass. Humans with walking sticks and backpacks have become completely and utterly boring to dogs that see your kind by the hundreds every day.

One morning, walking through a town so small it has no sign, a backyard gate into the alleyway opens and an old man and his dog appear. Suddenly, the dog tears past the man's legs, and he barks like crazy along the neighbors' fences. Then dogs on the other side jump up barking as well, and when their heads appear every second or two over the top, the noise escalates to a point where you want to cover your ears. The man goes to open the gates to those other yards and you think, is he nuts? What the heck does he think he's doing? You back against the wall of the building opposite, sure that there is going to be an intense dog fight with snapping teeth and flying hair. But the dogs spring through the gates only to jump around the man and lick each other, still barking with excitement, because they are so delightfully doggy happy to be going on their regular morning outing. You walk behind them for a while, watching their tails wag, with a grin on your face so big that your cheeks get tired.

You notice how much calmer you are with each day of walking. Your breathing has deepened and steadied, even when you're around a bunch of dogs. You feel like your world has gotten fuzzier for having them in it. You're sure that your favorite photo from the trip is going to be the one of the golden-reddish dog lying in the shade at the foot of a golden-reddish bank of dirt. The colors match so well that, at the time, you almost missed seeing the dog, except that a pair of sweet brown eyes met your own.

♦ THREE ♦

You spent last night at an albergue a few kilometers before Pamplona, and now you're enjoying a bit of sightseeing as you walk through the old city this morning. The arched stone bridge over the Río Argo and the uphill climb along ancient city walls have brought you into a maze of cobbled streets, and you imagine Ernest Hemingway here in the 1920s heading toward his favorite bar on the Plaza de Toros. You're actually glad you're not here in July for the running of the bulls, because after weeks on the trail, (you started in Le Puy, France) you are valuing peace and quiet over excitement and noise.

You marvel at the distinctive architecture and the charm of the plazas, and as you exit the last narrow shop-lined street of the old town, you see the beautiful Parque de la Ciudadela across the way. The camino runs alongside it for a few blocks, so you decide to walk a parallel route on the park's wide footpaths. They are lined with shaped hedges, statues of gods and goddesses, flowering fragrant trees and color-drenched gardens. You come to a cobblestone promenade, where a left turn will return you to the camino, but first you cross it to look over the wall on the far side of the walkway.

You end up spending the next half hour there, unable to take your eyes off the scene before you. The wall drops way down to a wide moat-like area, grassy on the bottom, and enclosed by another high wall on the other side. And roaming the green field are healthy and happy populations of romping miniature goats, crowing roosters and clucking hens, shimmying peacocks and seemingly unimpressed peahens, numerous guinea fowl and a small herd of prancing deer. You are so delighted that you motion to some other peregrinos approaching through the park.

"You gotta see this," you tell them, and you wish the camino went right along this wall so that everyone could enjoy it. You take a bunch of pictures with your cell phone and look forward to sharing them with others in the albergue later on.

◆ ◆ ◆

Chickens, cows, and cats – three Cs distinguish my favorite animal memories of the camino. Chickens provide part of the ongoing soundtrack of the trail. There are small farms all along the way, and the chickens seem to live a blessed life, roaming freely, scratching in the dirt, even walking the streets of small villages. That must explain why the eggs I sometimes ate for dinner (at home I eat eggs for breakfast, but in Spain, that was rarely an option) were so extraordinarily golden-yolked and rich flavored.

Chickens hold a special place of honor in Santo Domingo. There was a miracle, originally attributed to St. James in Toulouse France in 1080, which in the retelling over centuries, ended up being credited to Santo Domingo who lived in the 11th century in the town which now bears his name.

Domingo provided comforts and built infrastructure for peregrinos along the Camino de Santiago. It is said that among those pilgrims, in the years after his death, there was a German couple and their handsome son who stopped at an inn for the night as they made their way along the trail. The innkeeper's daughter took a fancy to the young man, but when he resisted her advances, she decided to get back at him. She snuck a silver cup into his knapsack. As he was leaving town the next day, she reported to the authorities that he had stolen it. The young man was captured and immediately hanged. But his parents saw that he was still alive, because the saint, James or Domingo depending on which version you hear, was supporting him under his feet.

The parents went to the justice, who was sitting down to a dinner of roast chicken, and told him that their son was alive and should be freed, because his innocence was proven by the saint's intercession. When he replied that, "Your son is no more alive than these chickens on my plate," the birds sprang up, good as new, and leapt off the table.

My husband and I walked into Santo Domingo early in the day on Sunday May 15, which just happened to be the final day of the Festival of Santo Domingo. The town was full of people enjoying live music, busy markets, a holy day Mass and a colorful parade along the street in front of the cathedral. The spectacle included young girls in traditional dress carrying baskets of vegetables, boys jumping and turning in choreographed patterns with castanets bouncing in their hands, priests swinging incense burners on chains, a statue of Santo Domingo carried on the shoulders of four men, and an all-ages band playing a slow processional.

Afterward, we gladly paid the pilgrim's price of 2.50 euros for entrance to the impressive cathedral/museum. The whole place is a work of art, the creamy marble of the building accentuating the rich colors of paintings and statuary. The ornate silver tomb of Santo Domingo holds center stage and can be viewed from above or below the main floor level.

But we had to look around for a while before we could find the chickens. What? Chickens? From the moment we entered the sanctuary, we could hear the cluck- cluck and the cock-a-doodle-doo of two live chickens, like those that came back to life in the story. There they were, tucked into an alcove above the saint's tomb, in what I assume is quite the chicken penthouse. Every 20-some days, new chickens are rotated in so that there are no health problems for the birds. I'm fascinated by the thought that, besides dusting statues of Mary and Jesus, sweeping flagstones, polishing gold fixtures, and wiping thousands of fingerprints from wooden doors and pews each day, the custodians of this church also give good care to chickens, keeping alive a thousand-year-old legend.

We left Santo Domingo at 7:30 the next morning after breakfasting on the chicken-shaped pastries we had bought the day before. At lunch time, we came to Villamajor del Río, the birthplace of Santo Domingo himself. There was a lovely town square with picnic tables, and we claimed one in the sun and started unpacking our crackers, cheese, and apples. A municipal worker was cleaning dirty water and algae out of the pool around the fountain, and the lone fish that called that concrete tank home was waiting in a wheelbarrow full of water set in the shade.

I pointed out to my husband that the four or five cats wandering the square weren't as skinny as many cats we'd previously seen along the way. Within minutes we found out one of the reasons why (although it's also possible that they found a way to help themselves to fish in the pool). Each cat in turn came to the area around or under our table, let out a single meow, then looked at us with big eyes, like Puss-In-Boots in the Shrek movies.

They were very polite little beggars and didn't make a

nuisance of themselves, so we decided we would give them each a bite of cheese once we'd finished eating. One of the cats meandered off to try his luck at the next table where a peregrino traveling with a small dog was taking a break. He swung his walking stick and yelled at the cat to get lost. Maybe he was worried that the cat would harass his poor tired dog.

The cat came back to our table, and when we had cut the last chunk of cheese into five delicate slices, we gave one to each cat. They took the cheese with the best of manners and didn't fight among themselves.

Cows walked the camino with us in Galicia quite a few times. Galician cattle are beautiful, tan and sleek, and never having walked right beside a cow before, I was a bit intimidated by their size and weight. Local farmers use the paths and roads of the camino to move their cattle from pasture to pasture, so much of the trail is paved with cow poop. That's just one of the good reasons why albergues have separate boot rooms near the entrances of the buildings – the other reason, I'm sure, has to do with the smells of hot feet which have soaked into the material of everyone's footwear.

A favorite camino memory is of the afternoon my husband and I sat on the patio of a charming café at a crossroads in Galicia called Eirexe. The patio was separated from the street by a long water trough, and a huge oak tree beside the trough shaded one half of the patio. Some peregrinos were sitting in the shade and some in the sun, and all were enjoying a late afternoon coffee or beer or wine. Suddenly a gate to the field next to the café was opened and five cows ambled into the street, lined up at the trough, and proceeded not only to slurp loudly (as your mother taught you never to do) but to raise their noses to the sky as they drank so everyone could see their throat muscles ripple as the water glug-glug-glugged down.

We drinkers on the patio held our cups or glasses halfway to our lips as we watched, feeling that our small measure of afternoon refreshment was, literally, just a drop in the bucket compared to the bountiful quenching of bovine-sized thirst we were witnessing. When the cows moved on, my husband and I raised our glasses and clinked a toast to them. Many more toasts followed as we sipped our way through an excellent bottle of wine, raising our glasses to cats, chickens, donkeys, horses, sheep, deer, storks, lizards, quiet dogs and any other animal we could think of that had increased the pleasure of our weeks on the camino.

THE FRUSTRATION CAMINO

♦ ONE ♦

You love maps. When you travel, whether it's by car with your road atlas on the seat beside you, or by canoe with the topographical map in its waterproof case tied to the thwart in front of you, you make your way through a landscape and across a page with continual cross-references.

As you walk the camino, the Rother Walking Guide is in your easiest-to-access vest pocket. You pull it out at least every half-hour to confirm the names of villages you see in the distance, to figure out if the trail goes up and over the hill ahead or if it veers off to the right or left, to determine how much longer you'll be walking beside the road, or to make an educated guess as to where and when you'll be able to sit down for a second cup of morning coffee.

It's funny to read the information about the country you're travelling through from left to right across the page but then, because you're hiking from east to west, to read the map section from right to left. To make it even more confusing, when those same towns which appear from right to left on the map are shown on an elevation-change graph, they are listed from left to right along a horizontal axis. You end up mostly disregarding the graph anyway because, although it might show only a slight elevation change between town A and town B, it doesn't show all of the steep little ups and downs that make you sweat and lean on your hiking stick along that stretch.

After some weeks of hiking, you reach Galicia, a breathtaking and enchanted part of Spain. Unfortunately for you, the enchantment seems to be quite literal and adversely affects the accuracy of the map. There must be little elves or wizards who change where the trail goes, the names or even the existence of villages, and the number of hills you have to walk up. In your Rother Walking Guide it clearly states that, after Hospital da Condesa, there's a serious climb to the top of the Alto do Poio, but that it is "the last big hurdle to Santiago." When you trudge up steep and long hills every day for several days thereafter, you realize you'll have to learn to laugh it off, or you'll have to leave the book in your pocket, because your frequent venting at the author of the book is starting to negatively affect your camino experience.

◆ TWO ◆

When you were in grade two, your whole class drew anti-littering posters. "Don't be a litterbug," yours said, and when all twenty posters were hung in a display case outside city hall, you thought no one would litter ever again.

You've taken part in beach clean-ups, and you keep the sidewalks and curb areas in front of your home and business spotless. You truly can't understand why people litter. Don't they see how ugly it is? Don't they care that they're disrespecting Mother Earth? Don't they know that littering is the eighth deadly sin?

You had hopes and fears about litter along the camino before travelling to Spain. Well, it's not as good as you hoped and not as bad as you feared. There is toilet paper on the ground along the trail and quite a collection of it in places where it's easy to go off behind some bushes. But at least in this climate it breaks down fairly quickly, so the mess isn't overwhelming.

Then things change as you get closer to Santiago de Compostela. A lot of people start their hikes near the 100 kilometer marker since walking that distance is the minimum requirement for earning a pilgrim's certificate. All of a sudden, the energy is more frenetic and less friendly. The noise level is higher. Trail markers and walls are scribbled with graffiti. And, oh dear, the litter is bad. Disposable water bottles, pop cans, and snack papers have been randomly tossed aside. In some wooded areas, there are trash barrels that you're guessing were put there by local landowners. Either the barrels are overflowing or they've been picked through by animals or they've been disregarded by hikers.

You had thought that peregrinos might be a pretty enlightened bunch about things like littering. But you realize that was unrealistic. The camino is a slice of life, and you're going to get goods and bads just like you do anywhere else.

♦ THREE ♦

You brought a tent, but it hasn't been worthwhile because most places don't allow camping. You arrive in a town at the end of a day, you're dead tired, and all you want to do is take a shower and put your feet up. Your Spanish isn't good enough to ask around for local options, so now you are staying most nights in albergues and sometimes take a break from people by getting a room in a hostal or pensión.

Albergues are a mixed bag. You find most of them quite pleasant, and sleeping in a roomful of people is easier than you thought it would be, even with occasional snorers.

The guidebook shows the location of many albergues and, since the camino has become so popular lately, new ones have opened up, and there's often a choice of places to stay. Many towns have a municipal albergue or a church-run refugio, and those are usually the cheaper options. Privately run albergues cost a few euros more, but you can expect some extras like sheets and towels or more room between bunk beds or nicer bathrooms.

So here you are in Mélide, and you've just handed over twelve euros for a bed in the private albergue that's across the street from the municipal one. That's the most you've paid so far. As the reception person shows you upstairs, you're unnerved by the metal stairway. It clangs and echoes like the inside of a jailhouse. The room she shows you is so jammed with beds that there is no room to put your pack beside your bunk. And for the fourteen people in this room, there is only one toilet, one shower and one sink. The woman hands you a cellophane wrapped package containing a disposable sheet and pillowcase, the same kind supplied in five-euro-a-night places.

Tiredness and a lack of Spanish lead you to feel unable to cope well with the situation. So you just cope.

◆ ◆ ◆

I substitute teach in elementary schools, and at the beginning of each school year, in math, there's a unit on patterns – recognizing them, creating them, continuing them. Patterns are very comforting in math and in real life. You know what to expect. In the adult world, they make systems more efficient and services more convenient.

I think, sometimes, that I should upset that curriculum just a bit by presenting a pattern then blowing it to smithereens. When I'd ask the kids how they'd deal with it, the lesson would become more like philosophy than math. Maybe it would be good preparation for hiking the Camino de Santiago.

For instance, let's look at the camino's salad pattern. Salads improved as my husband and I traveled west on the trail. Iceberg lettuce gave way to leaf lettuce, and more veggies were added like grated beets and corn. But the pattern didn't last, or should I say it didn't remain consistent. Sometimes iceberg lettuce came back, and sometimes veggies were sparse. The biggest upset to the pattern came in one café where tuna, a frequent addition to ensalata mixta, was replaced by ham. I picked it off and gave it to my husband since he's the red meat eater in our family.

Then there was the coffee break pattern. For quite a few days in a row, we walked seven or eight kilometers after breakfast and a bar would appear at the next crossroads, the espresso machine steaming a warm welcome. Then the pattern changed. For the next few days we had to walk ten to twelve kilometers for that second boost of caffeine, and that extra distance and time gave rise to faint headaches and grumpy moods. As we walked through villages leading up to the ten-to-twelve-kilometer café, I would think, why doesn't some business-minded person in this town open a little place that would cater to all the peregrinos walking by?

The wine pattern was wonderful for wine lovers. With a pilgrim meal, I'd request vino tinto or vino blanco, and I'd be served a large mug of wine or half a bottle just for me. If my husband and I ordered the same kind of wine, a full bottle or a pitcher would be placed on our table.

On my husband's birthday, we reached the town of Cee on the Galician coast. We walked to the plaza and saw a pilgrim meal advertized for eight euros including wine. So when ordering our red wine, we asked for a bottle. Later when I went to the counter to pay for the birthday dinner, the owner said, "Treinta y dos euros."

"Thirty-two euros? What?" Then I pointed at the sign and stumbled in Spanish, "Peregrino menú – ocho euros."

As he replied he held up one finger to illustrate "una copa de vino," one glass of wine. He then went to his wine rack and pulled out a bottle like the one we'd just drunk. He referred to it as "vino especial."

At that point I just dug into my wallet and paid. I didn't have the language facility to argue about what I'd asked for or not, or the expectations I'd had based on previous experience. Heck, I'd have had to consult my grammar book just to remember how to form the past tense.

I felt some sorrow as I told my husband what had happened – I didn't like the idea that a fast one had been pulled on me because I'm an ignorant foreigner. We agreed, though, that it was a real blessing that something like this had only happened once in a full month of travelling.

And that focus on blessings is just the kind of turn-around thinking that was perhaps my most important lesson on the camino. If I got upset about lack of consistency in food preparation and cost, infrequency of services, and less than 100% honesty among restaurant owners, then the problem did not dwell in the food, the pricing, the business locations and the human beings trying to make a buck, but in my totally imaginary vision of how things should be. I just had to not expect anything – piece of cake, right?

Well, until the next time. I was in Finisterre for two nights. The first evening, I walked along the waterfront between 5:00 and 5:30, and several of the restaurants were serving dinner already. I read the sign boards, chose one, and had a lovely meal of salad, fish stew and rice pudding. When I went back to that part of town the next evening at the same time, it was practically deserted. A few people were having a glass of wine, but there was no food to be seen, not even tapas. I went into the restaurant where I'd eaten the night before and tried to get information. The waiter, speaking so quickly I hardly caught a single word, pointed to the kitchen staff sitting at a table and eating a meal. I did manage to ascertain that dinner would not be available until 8:00. Really? Why? It was too much for me to handle gracefully on an empty stomach. I got myself into quite a funk as I walked to the grocery store for a container of potato salad.

THE QUIRKY CAMINO

♦ ONE ♦

The 2:00 sun is just on the verge of getting too hot when you stop for the day in Cacabelos. When that sun shines golden through the sheer white curtains of your second story room and you lie across the bed in its warm path, you fall asleep for a few minutes.

It's been one of those days on the camino when everything has gone right – the weather, the coffee, the company and now this town. It's big enough to have everything you need but small enough to make walking around a pleasure. There's even a rubberized jogging trail along the river. You walk on it and wish the whole camino were rubberized.

You and some friends have an afternoon drink at an outside table on the patio of a small café. It's right beside the camino, right near the river, right across from the old church. There's a paella sign out front, and that means you can have dinner any time you want. Perfect!

The owner is well-dressed, clean-cut, dark-haired and so hospitable. He brings small bowls of peanuts, pretzels and other crunchies to your table and replenishes them as you and your buddies snack them away. You smile at him and he smiles back as though he's having as much fun as you are. Something about him seems familiar.

You leave to run a few errands – bank machine, post cards, laundry-folding – then return for your evening meal. Along with a chicken paella you order the vino de casa, and he brings a bottle with a fancy pink label on it. You are skeptical, because a label usually means a higher price. You ask, "Cuánto cuesta?" and he says eight euros. That's more expensive than you're used to paying for house wine, but you agree to it, because you can tell he really wants you to try this particular wine. It's a local El Bierzo wine, and you've read about its good reputation.

He's like a live advertisement with his gesturing hands and expressive eyebrows. He magics a corkscrew from his pocket and opens the bottle with a flourish. The cork pops out, and he flips his wrist and waves the cork under his nose. His eyes close with pleasure. Then he places his left hand behind his back and pours some into your glass. You sip and now it's your eyebrows going up. It's the best wine you've ever tasted.

He beams and bounces on his toes. Just like Mr. Bean, you think. Oh, that's who he reminds you of!

Through the rest of the evening, you call him Mr. Bean in your mind. You watch him bustle, attend, nod, turn, present, twinkle. He's the best show on the camino, and when you get up to go, you leave a bigger tip than you usually do.

♦ TWO ♦

Somehow this morning, you feel as though you're sleepwalking. That's weird, because this section was supposed to be one of the high points of the hike, literally. The Cruz de Ferro stands at the highest elevation of any spot on the camino, and you've snoozed right past it. The light was dim for one thing. And like disturbing dream images, the sight of old shoes, discarded water bottles, crumpled notes and faded friendship bracelets accosted you there. So you lowered your head, kept it down, just looked at the path and went on by.

You've heard the view is great on the way down, but clouds are all you see. They remind you of the pattern on your bedsheets at home. You listen to your breathing like you do to help you relax into sleep when something is bothering you.

You find a good sitting rock, lean against the bigger rock behind it and eat your leftover toast from breakfast. You could be alone in a space capsule way up in the silent beyond. You could be a single grain of sand in the middle of the Sahara.

You brush breadcrumbs from your pants. It takes effort to pick yourself up, as if you're stuck in one of those dreams where you're weighted down, held by invisible bindings. You walk, step after heavy step.

Suddenly you startle awake. Is that an alarm clock? Is that someone snapping crisp sheets? You peer down the road, past a crumbling stone house and around the bend. There ahead is a little cartoon oasis, a dancing island of color.

A second crumble of stone house is surrounded by flags and banners flapping like wild partiers. Someone is standing among them ringing a bell and waving. Me? You gesture, pointing at your own chest. Sí, he nods and opens his arms like a circus ringmaster.

You find the uneven stone steps to his door amid pots and shrubbery and flag poles. By the time you reach the top, the man is handing you a steaming mug of café con leche. How did he know what you drink? It's wonderfully strong and starts blowing away the clouds in your brain, just as the mountaintop wind is dissipating the overcast. The sun reaches out to greet you.

The man is singing Beatles' tunes as he refills your cup, an unusual occurrence in Spain. You wander over to the signpost tree which has branches of arrows pointing in all directions telling you how many hundreds or thousands of kilometers you are from London, New York, Tokyo, Rio de Janeiro, Johannesburg, Moscow, Sydney. Oh yes, and one other sign points to the outhouse across the road, the only toilet facilities here in Manjarín.

The flags snap around you. The man rings his bell for the next group of approaching peregrinos. The coffee kicks in. You look down and notice how solidly your feet are connected to the ground. Your space shuttle has landed. Your grain of sand has dropped through the hourglass of time and settled in the now.

♦ THREE ♦

You thought the camino would be a serious endeavor, full of silence and reflection and inner processing. You didn't know there would be goofy things that would make you bust out laughing all along the way.

It's all innocent fun. There was the plastic figurine of one of the seven dwarves — you think it was Doc — peering out from beside a henhouse.

72

There was the stuffed Shrek sitting up in a tree branch above a garden wall. And then there were the giant welded metal ants cavorting on a lawn and the home-made green-faced peregrino dressed in the old clothes of the farmer whose land the camino traverses.

At some point, you realized that the quirky things you see along the trail don't distract you from your meditative journey. Somehow they deepen it.

You are reminded of your childhood when all the wonders of the world existed in your own yard – the smell of the lilacs, the segmented glimpses of sky seen from a lazy hammock strung between two tall oaks, the burst of light from a hundred fireflies that you and your brother caught, shut into the milk box, then dumped all at once onto the dark summer lawn. Then, as today, you've known without doubt that life's simple pleasures are the best.

And now you come upon one of the wayside camino markers which, along this stretch of trail, feature a little fox dressed in an old-fashioned pilgrim's cape, hat, and sandals. Someone with a Sharpie pen has added a dialogue bubble with the words, "¿Dónde estan mis pantalones?" "Where are my pants?" It's the kind of humor eight and nine-year olds really like. And it tickles your funny bone unmercifully.

◆ ◆ ◆

When my husband and I stopped in a bar or café for second breakfast or lunch, I tried to sit with my back to the television. When we first arrived in Spain, I thought about paying attention to the programs to try to improve my Spanish. But there's only so much pouty-lipped MTV teen sexuality, or shiny-shoed, perfect-haired, aren't-I-clever talk show personality I can stand.

But one day, there was a show I thoroughly enjoyed watching. I lingered over my cup of tea to see it all. It was a cooking show.

The special guests were three nuns – a tall robust young woman, a medium-sized middle-aged one, and a tiny withered grinning old crone who could barely be seen above the counter-top.

The young nun did most of the talking. She and the middle-sized one were layering ingredients – potatoes, meat, red peppers, egg, and a sprinkling of herbs. I think it was a specialty of their convent. The tiny old woman nodded and pointed and smiled.

At some point, she disappeared. Maybe it was her nap time. I imagined her curling up in a very small bed. The other two didn't seem to notice her absence as they continued their food preparation. Then the middle-aged nun left the set as well and never returned. I imagined her in a medium-sized bed. My husband said, "I wonder what's going on?" I shrugged.

The young nun put the finishing touches on the dish and set the culinary creation down on the counter. The camera zoomed in on her hands holding the edges of the dish. Then her hands went away. Off to siesta in a big bed?

I looked at my husband's quizzical expression. I said, "So now Goldilocks comes in, sees the food, declares it 'just right', and eats it all up." It turns out he didn't grow up with that story in his home country, so he had no idea what I was referring to. Talk about getting lost in translation! I could tell him what happened to Goldilocks but, alas, there was no way for us to discover the fates of the three disappearing nuns.

THE SENSORY CAMINO

♦ ONE ♦

You call them Basque horses, although you don't know if that is an official breed name. They're brown and sturdy and are the perfect horse for the Pyrenees Mountains. They move uphill and downhill, over steep pastureland, calmly and strongly as if the curves of their musculature evolved to match the lay of the land.

You wake up in the morning in Subiri hearing, through an open window, their bells jangling. You imagine their warm breath in the cool air condensing into visible puffs of fog. You stretch, willing your muscles and joints to adapt to the mountains as well as those of the horses have.

You walk the narrow streets after breakfast, heading back toward the arched bridge that brought you into town. You hear the unmistakable ringing clip-clop of hooves on paving stones and, as you turn a corner, you see a man leading horses on the road ahead of you. How many? You do a quick count – fourteen horses, some of them new foals beside their mothers. They're heading out to the pasture, and they seem excited as if this is a brand new experience rather than the routine they do every day of their lives. They toss their heads and dance their front legs when the procession slows momentarily. Let's go, let's move, they seem to say.

Walking the camino is like that. There's an excitement every morning, an urge to be on the way. Your muscles twitch and ripple with the anticipation of something. It's not the anticipation of newness, although you will, unlike the horses, pass through different terrain each day. Perhaps like the horses, you just look forward to experiencing what the world has to offer with an alert mind and a moving body.

The fourteen horses turn left toward their grazing area after crossing the bridge, and you and the camino turn right toward Pamplona. You walk past other groups of horses in other fields, on other hillsides. When they move along the fence lines, you feel the energy of the herd. They stretch their legs like one organism, turning this way and that. You sense how that energy gives a boost to the slower or weaker members. If you didn't have a pack on your back, you'd be tempted to pick up speed, try to keep pace. You feel color in your cheeks and the pulse in your neck.

There are other hikers around you this morning. You feel their energy, too. Their greetings are like the nickers and head-shakes of the horses. Their human legs move in rhythms that match your own, and their sturdiness encourages you to be strong and steady.

♦ TWO ♦

You've heard the science about smells and memory, how scents are strong triggers for recall. You walk the camino and can practically feel all of your sensory synapses firing in the presence of multi-hued fields and forests, birdsong and street music, and new foods and good wine. But you're pretty sure that what you will remember best thirty years from now is the smell of the grape flower.

Past acres and acres of twisty old vines you've come through the region of Navarre and into La Rioja. You wish you could watch the farmers prune the vines and learn the tricks for keeping gnarly stems so productive. Big green leaves emerge so fresh and supple, tinting the light that moves around and through them.

You smelled the flowers before you saw them. So sweet— like honey and fruit and babies' heads. They were hard to spot tucked under the leaf canopy and not showy at all. Parts of the flowers look like the fruit they will become -- miniature pale grapes splaying outward on delicate white pin heads. They remind you of tiny star bursts. You get your camera out and sit in the dirt, your head tucked under a grape vine to take the picture.

"Wouldn't it be cool if you could make scratch-and-sniff photos?" you say to your boyfriend.

"Shhh, c'mere, look at this," he says and motions you across the farm lane. As you approach, he points at the stone wall that runs along the edge of the field opposite the vineyard. There are olive trees and poppies on its far side, but he is looking at the wall itself. At first, you just see rocks and lichens and ivy, but then there is a movement. Then another. And another. Small brown lizards are crawling in and out and over and around each hole and crevice and protrusion. Once you know what to look for, you see them everywhere. When they pause to sunbathe, their long tails curve and conform to the shapes of the rocks beneath their bellies.

"I've never seen so many lizards in one place before," you say.

Your boyfriend whispers, "It's like the stones are alive."

When you see that he will be absorbed in watching them for a while, you drift back to the other side of the road. You put your nose close to a grape flower and inhale deeply. This scent should be bottled as a magic potion, you think. It makes you feel as refreshed as you do after a day at the spa. So you bottle up the memory of it and think, with pleasure, about uncorking it thirty, forty, maybe fifty years from now.

♦ THREE ♦

You step inside the church. It is cool here while outside it is hot. It is dimly lit while outside it is blazing. It smells faintly of incense while outside the smells are of mown fields and warmed pavement. It is very quiet. Any sound beyond the thick wooden doors is muffled.

This is a good place to be mid-afternoon. The heat and sun can suck the energy right out of you after about 2:00. The Spanish are smart to have siesta time. Peregrinos tend to keep going through the afternoon if they have a destination to reach. You find a church and take a break, for your body and your spirit.

Some churches are better than others for giving your senses a rest. The Iglesia de Santa María in Los Arcos is more the kind of place you go into to gawk. It's a dense mixture of architectural styles and Rococo adornment, all clamoring for your attention. "Whoa," you said the day you walked in its front door. You only stayed long enough to admire the workmanship and to let the sweat dry off your back.

In Triacastela, you declared the Iglesia de Santiago your favorite. The church was small and plain. You felt calm there, enclosed by smooth stone walls. There was a simple altar in front and just a few works of sacred art on the side walls. The light inside was golden that afternoon, and you didn't get a stiff neck gazing upward as you sometimes do in big Gothic cathedrals.

But now, you're near the end of your camino. In the evenings, you look back through your pilgrim passport at all of the stamps you've collected at albergues and churches along the way. Except for the two stylistically opposite churches in Los Arcos and Triacastela, the memories you have of other ones where you've stopped for afternoon breaks have blurred and overlapped. That's okay.

You're walking the camino to have time for God, and since God is everything and everywhere, you don't want to get hung up in the details. If, remembering back, you feel yourself sitting in a dark pew, your hands brushing along its smooth surface, then you have God in your fingertips. If you bring back the moment when your soul flickered to life in the light of the votive candles and glowed golden and rosy beneath windows of stained glass, then God is before your eyes. When you hear again, in the quiet part of your mind, a hush so large that it reaches into every lovingly constructed and ornamented corner of every church where it echoes infinitely, then it's God you've heard.

You close your eyes each night, lying on a narrow bunk, and give thanks for your body, a temple designed for holding God close. You give thanks for the trail outside the church doors, the path where you walk with God who is everywhere evident in the colors and shapes and sounds of the camino.

◆ ◆ ◆

If I had had a digital camera instead of a film camera as I

walked the camino the first time, I would have taken hundreds of pictures of doors. Until I hiked in Spain, I only thought of doors in utilitarian terms if I thought of them at all – a door should be solid, open and close quietly, fit its frame well, and have good locking mechanisms.

In Spain, the doors were like invitations. Come knock on me; come visit, they said. What do North American doors say? I want my privacy?

In some cases, the doors invited me with color – kelly green, aquamarine, brick red, always softened with age and married to the texture of the wood. The stone archways or block frames around the doors promised coolness within. The metalwork on older doors, horizontal rows of circular or filigreed bronze, communicated strength. And the heavy door knockers almost tempted me to play pranks; like children ringing doorbells and running away, I wanted to lift and let drop the solid hunks of metal and hear the boom resound through the house before, yes, running away.

Even the more modern doors had personality and distinction. On the front of one eye-pleasing house in Villamajor del Río, there were three doors. At the center of the structure was a solid door with a regular pattern of raised rectangles on its cedar-colored surface. The door was one step down from street level, and to each side of this entry way, along the pavement, were turquoise pots of all sizes, overflowing with flowering plants. Just above, and partially shading the center door was a small balcony with wrought-iron railings serving as uprights for climbing roses. Double doors, with tall slender windows in them, opened onto this Juliet-worthy lookout. The third door, at the right edge of the housefront, was at street level and had a curtained window in its top half that could swing open independently of the bottom half for conversation, bread delivery and neighborhood watch. I tarried as I walked by, wishing someone would poke their head out at that moment. I wanted to say Buenos Dias. I wanted to attach a human face to an architectural face that attracted me so much.

Just as the visual features of doors along the camino invited physical responses like touching, knocking or entering, I realized that my favorite music moves me to dance, and my favorite art inspires stories in my head. I imagine those busy neural pathways in my brain, like long and wondrous caminos. Where they cross and make connections to other senses, the sparking synapses are like doorways into places of joy.

THE ECONOMIC CAMINO

♦ ONE ♦

Your parents met, as they put it, bumming around Europe on $5 a day. When you were little, you watched their slide show so many times that you knew the stories by heart and almost thought they were your own memories. Those travel stories were part of parental lessons about how to deal with strangers, how to amuse yourself on days of bad weather, how to be observant when you're in strange situations, and how to save up your money and be frugal.

During your final year at college, you browsed the shelves of the university library and the main branch of the city library for updated travel books. A month or two abroad would be your graduation present to yourself. You knew there wouldn't be Europe-on-$5-a-day books, but you hoped for some $20-a-day guides. Forget it. One was called "Europe on a Shoestring," but the listings looked to you like gold-plated shoestrings. Even the cheapest accommodations were over $20.

One sentence caught your eye as you morosely flipped a few more pages, about to give up. It was in the Spain section, under "Activities." It said, "The Camino de Santiago (St. James Way) is perhaps Spain's best known trek." Well, walking is free, you thought. So you checked the camino out online. Suddenly, the wonderful possibility of cheap European travel unfolded before your eyes with each click.

Here's what you learned. Albergues, the places you sleep at night while on the camino, vary in price. The private ones can be a bit on the expensive side for a budget traveler, but some, run by religious orders, are by donation, and municipal albergues usually cost just a few euros.

Most albergues have kitchens where you can put together your own dinner, and some offer simple breakfasts of toast and coffee for next to nothing. As for dinner, nearby restaurants often advertise a peregrino menú, which includes soup or salad, a main course, dessert and wine for nine or ten euros. With these options and a bit of money for snacks in between, you can probably keep to about twenty euros a day which, although a bit more than twenty dollars a day, is still pretty good.

You can do this! It will be an adventure! And not just an adventure in terms of hiking through new countryside and towns every day, or of meeting people from all over the world and finding ways to communicate, or of getting in great shape while thinking about what you'll do with your life. You especially look forward to the adventure of taking on the challenge of cheap, like your parents did before you.

You picture yourself in Spain, asking, "¿Cuánto cuesta?" and commenting on items being "cara" or "barata", expensive or cheap. You imagine yourself walking with other young people, seeking out inexpensive places to stay and cooking together in communal kitchens. And you see yourself putting a twenty euro note into a small coin purse each morning and doing careful calculations throughout the day. You'll hold that little purse close to your heart as you count out small change.

You were glad you saw the big incense burner, the Botufumeiro, swing in the Martin Sheen / Emilio Estevez movie, "The Way", because you doubted you'd get to see it in real life. Friends who did the camino a few years before said they'd gone to three Masses, not very well attended, in the Cathedral of Saint James in Santiago de Compostela hoping to see the Botufumeiro. They learned that it was on display in the cathedral library and would only be swung on high holy days.

You figured it was a question of liability. In the past, it had twice broken loose, fallen among the congregation and killed someone. Your friends thought it was because it had turned into a tourist spectacle. People apparently applauded and snapped pictures -- and that during a church service, as if they were at a circus, for goodness sake.

So now, at the end of your camino, you are surprised and pleased when you arrive in Santiago and enter the cathedral for the noon-hour pilgrim's Mass, because there is the silver Botufumeiro hanging by a heavy rope from a high and sturdy beam above the altar. You quickly grab a seat, although you had planned to walk around first. Soon, the place is packed. Every seat is occupied, and people stand in all of the aisles. The peregrino beside you says the schedule of services when the Botufumeiro will be swung is on the church website.

You want to find out more, but a gentle voice comes over the P.A. system asking, in several languages, that people remain quiet in the sanctuary, and that photos only be taken without the use of flash. Well that part doesn't apply to you. You wouldn't even think of bringing a camera to church.

Once the service starts, everyone settles down. You don't understand much of the Spanish, but you enjoy hearing the long list of home countries of all the peregrinos who have arrived in Santiago in the last twenty-four hours. And you like listening to, and humming along with, the gentle smiling nun, who leads the singing in Latin.

After communion, the Botufumeiro is lowered and lit, and you realize you are holding your breath. The smoke wisps upward. Six monks in maroon robes cluster around the end of the pulley rope, and one priest moves forward, pulls the incense burner toward the side of the dais and pushes it gently, as one would a toddler on a swing.

One arc. Two arcs. Then just as the Botufumeiro passes the central low point of the third arc, the six men give a mighty downward tug on the rope, boosting it higher. This action is repeated at each pass until the 500 pound silver ball, now spewing scented smoke and crackling with flames, looks as though it might bump the ceiling or crash through one of the rose windows high on the walls of the transept. There are collective gasps you can hear even over the dramatic organ accompaniment.

You look around, and there are hundreds of cell phones and cameras tracking and recording the whole she-bang. You shake your head figuring the photographers are totally missing the grandness of the spectacle by watching it on three-inch screens.

Then the monks stop pulling and hold the rope steady. The Botufumeiro quickly loses momentum, but as it swings lower and lower, the organ music builds to a climax worthy of a heroic movie scene. Your hands tingle with the desire to clap, and you stick them in your armpits to control them. Then, to your amazement, as one priest catches and holds the Botufumeiro, and as the organist holds a final powerful chord, the tallest priest, with a big smile on his face, raises his hands in front of him, nods at the congregation with encouragement, and starts the applause. Everyone, including you, joins in.

In the evening, you join the 7:00 English-language tour, so you can ask questions. You thought the group would walk around the inside of the cathedral, but to your surprise, the guide leads you up hundreds of stone stairs, first to the high balcony where poor pilgrims slept in the old days, then out a small door and onto the roof. "Whoa," you say.

The group sits along the ridgeline of the nave while the guide points out the cross shape of the building, the towers of different architectural styles and purposes, and features of the modern city as compared with what one would have seen from up here during the Middle Ages. He leads you on a walk around the perimeter, from which you can see the cloister gardens, the bishop's residence and, most interesting of all, the stone casket-shaped receptacle where smelly and louse-infested pilgrims-of-old burned their clothes and felt themselves saved in more ways than one.

Then the guide beckons you around one last corner, and there you are, outside one of the rose windows you'd feared for during the swinging of the Botafumeiro. He says that the incense burner had, indeed, once broken through the glass, and you can't help taking a small step backward.

You raise your hand and ask about why the Botafumeiro is swung on some days and not on others. It's about money, he explains. People want to see it, but the quantity of incense it burns in one go is very expensive. Some tour companies or private individuals or church groups make donations to ensure the "performance," his word, happens on the day they'll be there.

You think back to the size of the crowd that afternoon. You remember the monks walking by every pew and among those standing in the aisles holding out cloth bags on sticks to receive bills and euro coins. You figure they must have taken in a few thousand euros in ten minutes time.

You know people who get upset thinking about the church and money. The history is ugly in places, especially when the church convinced the poor to buy forgiveness of sins and a ticket to heaven.

But there's the other side of the story. It takes a lot of people and resources to see to the well-being of the spirit, the community, and the art and architecture of churches. You don't have a problem with the finances of that reality. You're glad the swinging of the Botufumeiro contributes to the day-to-day expenses of running the cathedral in Santiago while, at the same time, giving peregrinos something they'll never forget, even if they didn't catch it on a three-inch screen.

♦ THREE ♦

You pride yourself on being a good money manager. You've never bounced a check or let your account balances drop below the level at which you'd have to pay extra fees. It's just addition and subtraction — no big deal. On the other hand, you don't get big-scale economics. It seems so circuitous, so deeply layered, so pumped up, so shady.

For months before your camino, you read all the newspaper stories you could find about Spain. Most of them talked about how bad the economy was — unemployed people giving up on the cities and moving to abandoned farms in hopes of at least being able to feed themselves; breeders of world-famous horses practically giving away their stock; young people demonstrating about the lack of jobs. You expected to see lots of beggars. You expected to see poverty-induced lethargy.

There are a few beggars in the larger cities, holding their hands out at the entrances and exits of major cathedrals. But otherwise, what you see is economic hustle and bustle. Bars and coffee shops and cafés are filled with the sounds of china clinking, espresso machines steaming, newspapers rustling, TVs babbling, and greetings and chatter cutting through it all. Bread delivery trucks squeeze along narrow streets, and the drivers carry bags of fresh crusty loaves to the doors of restaurants and private homes. Masons move huge stones from fallen-down buildings to the nearby sites of new homes, hotels, albergues, and eateries, bringing decrepit villages back to life. Farm markets set up in a different town each day and offer mouth-watering displays of fruits, veggies, cheeses and meats.

You keep in mind that you are only seeing one narrow strip of Spain, the string of communities linked by the Camino de Santiago. There's a micro-economy here that you can understand as well as your own bank books. It's simple addition and subtraction again.

Okay, maybe a little multiplication, too. Hundreds of peregrinos passing through towns every day, stopping and spending money in three to six of those towns for meals, snacks, drinks, groceries, accommodation, postcards and postage, cures for aches and pains and blisters, and replacements for worn-out or lost undies, socks and shoes. Additionally, coins go into donation boxes for votive candles in churches, the instrument cases of street performers and the hands of beggars.

You spend thirty to fifty euros a day within a space of twenty to thirty kilometers. Multiply that by, say, three hundred peregrinos, and that's 9,000 to 15,000 euros per day added to a 25 kilometer stretch of small-town economy. That's huge!

You love participating in finance on this scale. At home, it's mostly numbers on the pages of your credit and debit statements. Here, it's cash in the hands of people who are providing you with what you need. It's not circuitous or layered or pumped up, and it's definitely not shady. Best of all, you feel like your humble thirty to fifty euros a day is contributing to the economic recovery of a nation.

♦ ♦ ♦

Sometimes I think there's a gene for business sense. We all know individuals who have it. But it occurs to me there are also certain populations that seem to have the gene. I'd seen this distinction right at home among some First Nations of northwestern Canada. One band, the Tlingit, have traditionally been assertive traders between the Alaska coast and inland, between white merchants and native peoples. That propensity and talent for business continues to this day.

The same seems to be true of the Maragatos who live in the stretch of Spain between Astorga and Galicia, which the camino passes through. Their heritage comes from Berbers of North Africa who arrived during the Moorish invasion of the eighth century, Celts originally from the British Isles who settled in Galicia as early as 700 B.C., and Phoenicians, from the area of modern-day Lebanon, who, for a thousand years, dominated trade in the Mediterranean. This mix of well-travelled peoples in a natural transportation corridor gave rise to a distinct business-savvy culture. By the 16th century, Maragatos were known for carrying goods far and wide by mule train. It was Maragatos trading at the Galician coast who recognized the business potential of the first shipments of chocolate brought back by conquistadors from Mexico. They transported wagonloads to Astorga, their capital, where the beans were toasted over a wood fire, hand-peeled, ground, and melted slowly with sugar and cinnamon. To this day, Astorga is famous for its traditionally made confections.

My husband, a choco-holic who'd enjoyed sampling the city's goodies, and I headed out of Astorga one bright and chilly morning and noticed the differences in landscape and vegetation right away. It reminded us of the Scottish Highlands – definitely not farmland. I was impressed not only by the beauty of the purple-heathered slopes but by the neat and well-laid out villages.

We stopped in one for our usual second breakfast after about two hours of walking. We set our packs in the sun by an outdoor table, and my husband reminded me we had apples and crackers and cheese, so I headed inside planning to just order our hot drinks. I was back in a flash, telling him to forget the crackers and cheese. "You have to come see this," I said.

The counter was loaded with artfully prepared and arranged food – empanadas and bocadillos stuffed with fresh meats, cheeses, and veggies, numerous mouth-watering pastries and quiche-like pies and bowls of fresh fruit. Suddenly there was a line-up behind us -- the rumor of great food must have rippled back along the camino. The woman running the place seemed to have six hands as she poured teas and coffees and glasses of juice. She passed out plates to those wanting food, and they helped themselves. She kept track of who had what, who needed what, and who had paid and who hadn't. All the while, she sang along with the music playing in the background and smiled.

When we reached, within an hour, the next Maragato village, some friends from the Netherlands sitting at an outdoor table told us we had to stop. This, they said, as they pointed to their left, was the best coffee shop on the whole camino. We placed our hands on our still-full bellies and told them that was impossible. We'd just been to the best one.

And so it continued. That evening's dinner in Rabanal was a best. The hotel room in Molinaseca was a best. And the local El Bierzo wine was worthy of all the superlatives in my Spanish grammar book.

I don't have the business gene myself. But I recognize it when I see it. I'm happy to give my business to those who do have it and to provide all the free word-of-mouth advertising that I can.

THE LIFE AND DEATH CAMINO

♦ ONE ♦

How long have you known you would not make it to Santiago? Perhaps it's been evident for the past five slow days since you stood on the plateau of Monte Irago. You looked up at the Iron Cross on its tall oak post and wished with all your heart that you could climb it and continue upward to heaven. Or the idea may have fixed itself in your mind earlier, on the night you stayed at the Monastery de San Marcos in León and saw the Virgin Mother in a dream. She was beckoning to you. Or was it in Hornillos, a day and a half west of Burgos, when fellow travelers took you to a pilgrim hospital in hopes that the nuns could ease your constant shivering? Then again, you may have known already, when you left your home in Obanos.

All your life, you'd seen the cloaked pilgrims who had crossed the Pyrenees at Somport meeting those who'd come through Roncesvalles at the junction in your town. Your wife always said she felt blessed by the presence of peregrinos on a spiritual journey. You felt annoyed and overrun by dirty needy humans and their noisy beasts of burden.

Then, not long ago, your strong sons took over most of the farm work, your dear wife died, and you started coughing. You told your sons it was to honor their mother that you would make the pilgrimage to Santiago. You told them the cough was nothing.

But for the past five days, every breath has burned. You've measured progress by the shaky placement of your stick and your small shuffling steps beside it. You're cold; you're hot. Your skin is dry; your skin is clammy. You eat crumbs because your brain tells you to, but your body rejects eating as one more bother.

You had never heard of Villafranca del Bierzo when you were home in Obanos. But during the past few weeks, perhaps since Hornillos, the monks and nuns who have provided food and shelter for you along the way have also provided emotional comfort by telling you about Villafranca del Bierzo, which they call "Small Compostela."

Now, you've arrived. You saw the roofs of churches, monasteries and pilgrim hospices as you walked down the hill into town. But you seek only the Iglesia de Santiago which the good Brothers and Sisters gently suggested as a destination. You stand before that church's solid arched door, the Puerta del Perdón – The Gate of Forgiveness. By passing through, you will receive all the indulgences you would if you were able to reach Santiago.

You breathe and ready yourself. You raise your eyes to the carved figures overhead, witnesses to your salvation. Your vision blurs, and one of them looks just like you, like someone who can go no farther, standing beside and being supported by Jesus. You cry with relief knowing that when you pass through this door, your sins will be washed away and you will be spared the last difficult hundred miles to the Cathedral of St. James. You only need walk a few more steps with Jesus at your side, pass through this earthly portal and on toward everlasting life. And you'll gladly leave this sick and weakened body behind.

94

During your working life in Japan, you only had one week holidays. You and your wife did some of those whirlwind tours of Europe, North America and South America. Slowing down in retirement has taken some practice. You've taken up walking and photography. You are doing both with pleasure as you begin hiking the Camino de Santiago, and you have two months set aside to accomplish it.

It is April, and in southern France, as at home, the fruit trees are blooming. The petals drift as the fruit starts to form. In your own backyard in Japan are three plum trees that litter the lawn with a whiteness as soft as snow. Spring is your favorite time of year, and you usually would not choose to be away from home during this season, but your body doesn't deal with heat as well as it did when you were younger, so you want to make it to Santiago before the summer heat sets in.

Skies were blue yesterday when you walked uphill out of St. Jean Pied-de-Port on the Route Napoléon. You tied your light jacket around your waist. You pre-booked a bed at the Auberge Orisson so that you wouldn't overdo it on your first day, and you spent a comfortable night there.

This morning, the sky clouded over and the wind picked up. You layered your clothing and put on hat and gloves. You hope you'll still have some good views to photograph. Yesterday's were spectacular.

But by the time you've walked ten kilometers and climbed 700 meters in elevation, it is blowing snow and you can barely see the trail markers. You almost missed the one that leads away from the road and over the pass. Younger hikers have scurried past you saying, "Yea! We're in Spain now!" and asking if you're doing okay. You've smiled and waved and told them you'll see them in the albergue in a few hours.

You stop and get your sleeping bag out of your pack. You're already wearing all the clothes you have with you. Your rain gear is not doing a good job of blocking the wind. You'd rather keep your sleeping bag dry, because you've been motivated by the vision of reaching the albergue, stripping off wet clothes, taking a warm shower, and curling up in it on a bunk bed and feeling your body heat win the battle against the chill.

You realize suddenly that you don't know when you saw the last yellow arrow. The snow, blowing horizontally across the ground, is erasing shapes and edges. You retrace a few of your footsteps, but the rest are rapidly disappearing. Then you begin to walk squares – ten steps followed by a ninety-degree left turn and repeated three more times, then fifteen steps for the second square and twenty for the third.

This last square has brought you to a cluster of boulders. You squeeze in among them where the wind is partially blocked. You can't be far from the trail. Maybe you'll hear people walking by. Maybe visibility will improve and you can move on. If that fails, the young folks who passed you will send help back up the trail when you don't show up within a few hours. You may have to wait, but it will be light for quite a while yet.

You wrap the sleeping bag around your head and body, squatting with your back against a rock. Your body heat is not winning the battle against the cold. You try to imagine the snow as drifting plum blossoms. You try to remember it's spring.

♦ THREE ♦

Some strong distilled alcoholic drinks are called aqua vitae, the water of life. You've pointed this out, pretending it's an argument in your favor, when friends and family members have expressed concern about your drinking. You wish they wouldn't worry about you. You're holding down a job. So far, you haven't called in sick too often.

When your sister asked you to hike the camino with her, you got defensive right away. Was she trying to change you? Then she hugged you. She's the one who's always shown you that she loves you. She said if she wanted to get you away from alcohol, she wouldn't be inviting you to Spain.

Sure enough, alcohol is everywhere. Every coffee shop and restaurant is also a bar. Locals and peregrinos often have wine or beer with lunch and dinner and any time in between. You've seen a few having a beer at morning coffee break time. On the other hand, you haven't seen anyone drunk. You figure if you drink like the Spaniards do, three good things will happen. One – no one will worry about you. Two – you won't embarrass your sister. Three – you might learn to drink alcohol as if it were, indeed, the water of life rather than what some of your loved ones have suspected in your case – a death wish.

You have promised yourself you will not drink anything but coffee, water and juice until you and your sister are done walking each day. You will take a shower, change clothes and hang laundry to dry before heading to the bar even though by this time, you will want a drink so badly your teeth will hurt.

At home, you order beer by the pitcher. Here, you are trying a different drinking style. Like your sister, you order one glass of wine at a time. You take small sips. You set the glass down in between.

Your sister's limit is two glasses of wine, and you want to copy that as well. But you've been cheating – getting drinks on the way to the restroom, joining people at another table with the claim that the drink in your hand is your first, having a shot of something added to your coffee during the day.

Now you are in Mélide. You find the town depressing, and your feet really hurt. You and your sister are within a couple days walk of Santiago, and you have mixed emotions about that. It will be a great feeling of accomplishment to get there, but something great will be ending, too. What is it about walking the camino? It's the camino vitae, you think, grinning at your own joke. Then, as with many jokes, you realize the truth in it. It really is the camino of life. When before have you felt so fit, so interested in everything around you, so moved by people's stories? When, previously, have you thought of that first sip of alcohol each day as a celebration of what's good rather than a drowning of what's bad?

At home, you defined "really living" as seeing the room tilt and spin, talking and laughing loudly, having fuzzy feelings about everyone who shares a pitcher with you, forgetting for a while that neither you nor the world is perfect.

Now, in Mélide, you sit across a restaurant table from the sister who loves you. She offers a toast to health and happiness, and you each take a sip then set your glasses down. The food comes, and it is warm and filling. When you sigh, your sister looks up.

"You okay?" she asks.

"More than okay," you say. You reach for her hand. "Isn't life amazing?"

♦ ♦ ♦

As I walked the camino, the idea came to me that I was practicing for death. That's weird, I thought. Who practices for death? And what triggered that notion?

It might have come from the act of pilgrimage itself. There are a whole bunch of people walking the same path toward the same destination. Similarly, we're all walking the path of life toward its natural ending, death.

It could have something to do with all of the memorials to peregrinos who have died along the trail. You get it that death can come at any moment to anyone.

There are also lots of crucifixion statues along the way. Jesus's death and St. James's death a few years later have produced a world religion and inspired this particular pilgrimage trail.

A number of writers in the past few centuries have referred to death as the great equalizer. I also saw the camino as a great equalizer. Everyone, whether rich or poor, sane or crazy, lost or found, spent their days on the camino walking, eating, sleeping and dealing with discomfort. That's what I could outwardly observe, while also realizing that each individual's camino experience is unique. In the same way, I'm guessing that everyone's experience of death reflects their own singular attitudes about life.

When I've imagined dying, I've figured that it's better not to fight it. After all, there's no way to win that battle. The camino was good practice in that regard. I was in pain daily. I sometimes felt weak and discouraged. I felt loneliness, even with my husband at my side and peregrinos all around me. And I knew that I was likely to feel those things the next day and the next and the next, until I reached Santiago. I saw my choice. I could get tight and toughen myself up, or I could get soft and accept. Choosing the latter seemed the wiser when I realized that the pain, discouragement and loneliness I was feeling on the camino could be peanuts compared to what I might feel at the end of my life. If I fight those feelings now, I reasoned, they'll also get tighter and tougher, and they'll beat the crap out of me later, for sure. I'd rather die calm and peaceful than cursing and scrapping. I'm going for dignity on the deathbed.

I also don't want to die feeling regret and dissatisfaction. The camino had a great way of teaching me how to get past those bitter emotions. It made me work so hard climbing, trudging, sweating, hefting, balancing and adjusting, that whatever life on the trail handed me – a stone bench, a lukewarm shower, a creaky bed, a roomful of snorers, a grocery store the size of my closet with less than twenty items on its shelves, a bathroom without toilet paper, a long line-up at the coffee shop – could still be recognized as a gift rather than being deemed an annoyance to raise a fuss about. It was a case of seeing the glass half full rather than half empty. In weak moments, I admit I vented and fussed, but I found out that it was the fuss that made me feel dissatisfied and bitter, not the thing itself. The thing just was what it was. Life is just what it is. The camino is just what it is.

And what comes after? Ahhh, one of the great mysteries. What comes after death? Heaven? Sleep-like darkness? Enlightenment? Rebirth? For some reason, this question and its possible answers have never occupied my thoughts to any great degree.

But while walking, I did think a lot about what would come after the camino. Once my husband and I should reach Finisterre, the end of the earth, situated at the Costa da

Morte, the Coast of Death, what then? I didn't want to keep walking because I needed to let my knees and feet heal, but I didn't want life to just go back to normal. I wondered how I could hang onto the spirit of the pilgrimage.

Two things have happened since I returned home that have helped address that concern. One is that the spirit of the pilgrimage has firmly kept its hold on me. All I have to do is remember walking across Spain, and I feel bigger, calmer and more alive. The second is that I find myself imagining people, unknown individuals, thousands of them, walking the camino right this minute and tomorrow and next week. Pilgrim life continues even when I'm not there experiencing it, and that is comforting to me. It's kind of like eternal life.

THE EXPEDITED CAMINO

♦ ONE ♦

For a few months before you left Norway to walk the Camino de Santiago, you took long training walks every weekend – three to four hours of hills and valleys. You wore your hiking boots and your backpack, and into the pack you stuffed heavy wool blankets and a few large books for weight. When you got on the plane to fly southward, you felt prepared and fit.

But your pack is heavier now than it was with the blankets and books in it, and the trail is rougher than you thought it would be. The stress on your back and legs is so intense that you've thought about calling it quits every day for the last four days. You are hiking alone, and you recognize that you cannot continue without some help. You've gazed with envy at women putting water bottles into their husband's packs, at bicyclists with panniers, at a couple walking unencumbered beside a pair of pack donkeys.

As you register in the albergue that evening, you see a sign for Jacotrans baggage carrying service. For a few euros, a van will pick up your pack at the beginning of the day and deliver it to wherever you plan to stay at the end of the day. This will require extra planning on your part. You will need to set aside part of each evening, after doing laundry, writing in your journal, and finding a meal, to research in your guidebook or online for your next-day's destination, calling to make reservations, and filling out a bag transfer form.

Before your trip started, you would have thought of this as cheating. Now it seems more as if you're inviting a guardian angel to join you on the camino. You are so relieved that you will be able to keep going without the torture of carrying a backpack that you start to cry. You've been trying, for the past four days, to tell yourself that it would be okay if you couldn't make it to Santiago, but you know it wouldn't have been okay at all.

♦ TWO ♦

You've been looking forward to reaching Burgos later today. You hear that the old city is delightful, and you're going to take a much-needed day off. Your feet are sore and swollen. There was quite a lot of rocky up and downhill walking this morning, so at first when the trail put you onto the shoulder of the road, it was a pleasant change and the walking was easier.

But now you've walked kilometer after kilometer on the pavement, and the outskirts of Burgos are ugly. The afternoon sun is hot, and as you walk a long tree-less stretch past an airfield, you calculate that you only have seven or eight more kilometers to go for the day. That you can manage.

After two more kilometers, still on the pavement, still in the heat of the day, with feet more tender with each step, you see a sign that says you're still ten kilometers from the old town. The avenue that heads *toward city center is wide and straight, packed with traffic, and lined with plain concrete apartment buildings and factories.*

There is a bus sitting at a stop a few blocks ahead. The peregrinos who've been walking ahead of you for most of the morning board the bus, and you think, with hope, that if the bus is still sitting there when you reach it, you will hop on, even though your plan was to walk every step of the camino.

The bus pulls away from the curb well before you get there, and you realize that in that previous moment of hope, your plan changed. Screw walking every step of the way. This day has been too much for you already, and you cannot face another ten kilometers of hard plodding.

You walk into the lobby of a small hotel by the bus stop, say "Buenas tardes" to the receptionist, put your thumb and pinkie to the side of your head like a phone, and say, "¿Taxi?"

She nods, makes the call and says, "¿Veinte minutos?" Yes, no problem. Absolutely. You will gladly wait twenty minutes.

When the small cab pulls up, the driver lifts your pack into the trunk. You sit in the middle of the back seat with your trekking poles across your lap. The driver tells you a bit about what you're passing on the way and about the city. You understand about half of what he's saying. Mostly, you are nodding and smiling because you've never before enjoyed riding in a car half as much as you're enjoying this ride.

(Later you learn that there was an alternative trail that forked off before the airfield and followed the path of the river through parkland into town. You wish the signs had been better so you could have considered that friendlier option for approaching the city.

THREE

You like being part of a group. At home, you ride your horse at the arena with other women. You belong to a quilters' club. You prefer paddling a raft down a river with seven other people rather than a solo kayak. So it made sense to you to sign up for a guided tour of the Camino de Santiago. In years past, when you went to London and to Machu Picchu, your ex-husband planned the trips. Well, he's not around now, and you know what? You are going to have a great time anyway.

There are twenty-four people in your group from all over North America, mostly in the forty-five-to-seventy age range. On the first day, you all got royal blue fleece jackets with a Camino de Santiago emblem on the front. Some mornings it's pretty nippy, so you're glad to have it. It'll be a nice souvenir, too.

Each day, a bus takes you and your fellow travelers to a starting point like Roncesvalles or Nájera or Rabanal. The most scenic and most culturally significant sections of the camino have been chosen for this tour package, and you appreciate not having to walk through industrial areas or near military training zones. Life is hard enough without doing hard stuff on your vacation, too.

The bus meets you some hours later and takes you to a restaurant for lunch. The afternoons include a museum visit or other sightseeing. Atapuerca was really interesting. There's ongoing archaeological research taking place there about the earliest remains of humans found in Europe.

So this trip is perfect. You love to walk, and you're walking. You love to learn, and you're learning. You love making new friends, and there are twenty-three interesting people sharing this time with you.

But at the beginning of each day's walk, you either sprint off ahead of the others or take a long bathroom break just as the rest of the group sets out. You're not going to admit it to anyone, but you have an imaginary friend to walk with. Where the heck did she come from?

You think maybe she was real, that she was here 700 years ago. So many details about her come to you as you walk, sensing her by your side. She was from a port city in the Netherlands. The date 1327 pops into your mind. It was a plague year. She and her husband ran a tavern and their only son helped. When the son died of the black sickness, her husband went into a rage and blamed her. He was drinking all the time. She was afraid he would kill her. She told the neighbors she was going on a pilgrimage to grieve for her beloved son and to ask forgiveness for her sins, but she snuck out without saying a word to her husband and had no intention of ever going back. Across the centuries she tells you you're lucky to have gotten rid of your husband so easily. Divorce sounds like a piece of cake, she seems to say.

When you climb onto the bus at the end of that day's trail section, you imagine her waving to you. Wherever you walk tomorrow, she'll magically be there. She helps you see how spoiled you are in the twenty-first century. You wrap your blue fleece jacket around your shoulders as she wraps her long wool cloak around hers. The bus winds through the countryside, and you find yourself rocking to the comforting rhythm of easy travel. You look around at the others in your group and start to truly enjoy the banter. Over dinner you join in laughter and conversation. But you change the subject when anyone suggests walking together the next day.

◆ ◆ ◆

It was as I neared Logroño, about 165 kilometers into my camino, that I seriously thought I should quit. My feet hurt so badly by the end of each day that approaching a reception desk of an albergue or hostal was like walking on a bed of hot coals without the benefit of being in an altered state of consciousness. Every evening, my knees were so swollen it looked like I had inflatable neck pillows wrapped around them. And during the day, while walking, I was starting to experience sudden sharp pains as if tiny evil sprites were stabbing me in the calves, ankles, and sensitive parts of my feet.

My husband opened our camino guidebook to read the Logroño page. I tried to express interest despite my discomfort. It was mid-morning, so we wouldn't be stopping for anything more substantial than a snack, but we liked to be in the know about cultural sights we should keep our eyes open for.

"There's an Iglesia de Santiago here, "he said. "Shall we stop?"

"Yes," I said, getting a sudden inspiration. "I have something to ask St. James since we're walking his trail."

We found the church and went in quietly, leaving our packs by the door and sitting in a dark pew near the back. As an adult, I haven't been a regular church-goer, and having grown up Protestant, I'd never addressed a saint before. But I asked St. James if I should quit, if I should just give up on finishing the camino. I told him I didn't think the torture was worth it. One heartbeat later, the thought came to me to take what I'd learned so far about how to take care of myself while backpacking, put it into daily practice as far as Burgos, another 120 kilometers from here, and then decide. That seemed like eminently practical advice to me, so that's what I did.

And you know what? It really seemed to be working. Three or four days before Burgos, I was feeling so good that I was looking forward to setting out across the meseta on Burgos's far side. But my improvements proved temporary, and the day I walked into Burgos, I was half, no quite a bit more than half, crippled.

My husband and I booked ourselves into a small hotel for two nights, but recuperation was very slow. I knew that if, in the weeks ahead, we had to reduce our daily walking distances and take more days off, we wouldn't make it to Santiago in our allotted time.

I determined that I could handle getting crippled one more time but no more than that. I looked at the map to figure out where we could renew our journey that would still give us a respectable chunk of hiking to do, but that would be a distance I knew I could manage even if it meant hobbling to the finish line. I pointed on the map to O Cebreiro, a mountain-top world heritage site where the Celtic influence in northwestern Spain is clearly seen in the oval stone huts with thatched roofs. It's located 152 kilometers east of Santiago.

So we took the bus the next day to León, and I made sure to watch other peregrinos from the bus window when the camino paralleled the bus's route. I imagined myself walking with them through the flat wheat fields toward the endless horizons of the meseta. After an overnight touristy stop in León, we took a second bus across the hillier landscape to the west of the city and up the steep incline of the Galician mountains to the tiny town of Piedrafita. We got off there and walked four kilometers up a road to join the camino again in O Cebreiro. It felt so good to be back.

As we neared Santiago de Compostela seven days later, having covered the distance without any major physical problems, we spoke to an Asian man taking a break at a good photo-op location. He seemed pleased and proud as he stated that he had walked every step of the way. When I mentioned that I had needed to bus part of the way, he shrugged and smiled. "Well, that's the camino. It has to be a common-sense camino," he said.

THE GIFT OF SELF CAMINO

You've always had a thing about rocks. You carried them in your pockets when you were a kid, and touching them calmed you. Sometimes on laundry day, you'd hear a rattle-clunk in the dryer, and you'd race your mom to the machine so she wouldn't chuck your treasures out the back door.

Your sister had a flower garden of zinnias and marigolds. You had a rock garden. When your neighbor built a stone wall, you offered to help and got strong pushing the heavy wheelbarrow back and forth, got rough hands working with the concrete. You painted rocks to give to people as Christmas presents and asked your parents for stone carving tools as their gift to you.

The first time you saw pictures of inukshuks in a book about the Inuit people of the Arctic, you felt like you were falling backwards in time to one of your past lives. Your fingers tingled as though they remembered stacking slabs of stone into forms that served as signposts for a far-flung people. From that day on, you couldn't see an interesting rock without picking it up and placing it on top of another.

As you walk the camino, you have to control yourself. There are so many rocks that if you gave them all your usual amount of attention, you'd walk less than five kilometers a day. You force yourself to notice the sky, the birds, the trees, the churches, the farmers, the grapes on the vine, the signs to places you've never heard of before.

But once a day, as a treat to yourself, you build an inukshuk. Sometimes it's a small one on top of a sturdy trail marker. Sometimes you make a larger one at the side of the trail and stack the rocks into an almost human shape with one stone arm pointing west toward Santiago.

One morning, you wake up early and head out before others. You walk for half an hour beneath trees that dim the pre-dawn light. Then there's a breath of sunrise breeze, and the trees whisper a farewell as you emerge onto a curve of open hillside. The right side of the trail is a tumble of rocks tinted pink by light. The next thing you know, you've tossed your pack aside and are kneeling among them. You build inukshuk after inukshuk, and to you they represent the sky, the birds, the trees, the churches, the farmers working in their fields, and so much more. The peregrinos among whom you've been walking for the past three or four days are all passing by, but you keep stacking stones until the tumble of rocks has been ordered into a monument to the camino.

You pull out your phone to take a picture, but it's hard because your fingers are tingling so much. The rest of you is hungry and tired, so you decide to stop in the next town. That means you'll have walked just barely five kilometers. But in this one day, you feel as though you've covered the ground of several lifetimes.

TWO

You pass a lot of people on the camino as you walk, and yes, you realize you are the passer because you are twenty-two and haven't had any big injuries during your sports career, knock on wood. You know you've been lucky. You're thankful to the coaches you've had, who encouraged you and set reachable goals. As you pass peregrinos who appear to be discouraged or struggling, you wish you could give them a boost the way your coaches did for you.

At first, you thought about writing upbeat comments or drawing funny pictures on the walls of underpasses, the only place you ever do graffiti. You did a few, but you have to admit you find the amount of graffiti along the trail a bit disgusting. People have drawn on, and frequently made a mess of, all kinds of surfaces – walls, rocks, trail markers and signs. So for a few weeks, your pens have just stayed in the bottom of your pack.

That was until the day you walked by a tired-looking couple reading a sign about an upcoming albergue. "I wish they'd tell us how far it is," one said.

You thought of your coaches and reachable goals. Toward the end of a day of walking, you've noticed that peregrinos sigh or moan if they have six or more kilometers left to walk, but if it's five or less, they nod and say, "That's doable."

So you've pulled out one pen, the black one, and keep it in your pocket. On advertising signs or city limits signs or route signs, you add a small tag at the bottom that says "5 kms." You hope it will playfully remind people of what adults say when kids ask, "How much farther?" You hope it will make them laugh. You hope, especially, that it will make them see every destination as doable.

♦ THREE ♦

Your dear wife, your esposa, died suddenly just before Christmas a few years ago, and you felt deep despair facing the season alone. The two of you weren't much for socializing or going to festive events, but you had your own traditions. You always took a day trip in early December to Astorga to buy special chocolates and treats for the holidays. You played carols on the piano each evening and sang in two-part harmony. You went to midnight Mass on Christmas Eve and sat in one of the rear pews holding hands. And you set up an elaborate crèche in your front garden that included fresh hay in the manger and pine boughs along the stable walls with sprigs of dried flowers tucked into them.

Your home is at the edge of town, right alongside the Camino de Santiago. Very few pilgrims pass through in the winter. But when your wife was alive, those hikers who braved the season often stopped to snap a picture of your crèche. Your wife loved that. She poked her head out the door to wish them Feliz Navidad and Buen Camino then bustled out to offer a chocolate.

Since her death, you haven't wanted glances toward your grief-filled home. But now, in her memory, you want to set up the crèche, to offer treats. You know just the spot. You and she took regular morning walks along the camino trail going away from town. She marveled, over the years, that the two of you had walked the distance to Santiago several times, back and forth on this one stretch. You always turned around at the same place, by a huge old pine you called the Grandfather Tree – The Abuelo Tree. You placed your hand on the bark in greeting each time and felt sheltered and soothed in return. The figures of Baby Jesus, Mary and Joseph would be at home under that tree.

Into your garden cart you place the three-sided stable and the figurines. You put in some extra lumber and tools, a permanent marker, three

113

bowls and three bags from your last shopping trip to Astorga. It's a slower than usual walk to the Grandfather tree with the extra weight and the trundling cart, and your hands get cold.

When you reach your destination, you stand with your fingers tucked into your armpits to warm them. Just then, the low winter sun comes out from behind a cloud, and a ray of light shines on the spot at the base of the tree where the manger scene will stand. It's like the star of Bethlehem, you think -- confirming the wonder, highlighting the miracle.

You build a low stand and a peaked roof over it. You set the crèche within the structure and add dry grasses and pine boughs. You gently place the figurines in their usual spots, but you give the three Wise Men extra space for the bowl that will go in front of each of them.

You take out the marking pen and label the first bowl "Gold." You pour small gold foil-wrapped chocolates into it. The second bowl, labeled "Incense," you fill with licorice sticks that remind you of sticks of incense — probably not the form in which it was presented to Baby Jesus but, oh well. Myrrh, another fragrant resin, you have chosen to represent in its blobby form with caramel toffees. You feel your wife smiling down on you from heaven.

You walk again to the Grandfather tree on New Year's Day, once again pulling the garden cart. You'll take down the crèche and store it away until next year. You're glad to see that the bowls are empty and hope it's not due to squirrel theft.

As you pick up the manger and pull out the dry grasses, small coins spill around you. It takes you a moment to realize that passing peregrinos have responded as they would to a donativo stand and have left an offering in return. "Gifts from the Christ Child," you whisper.

So you change your mind. You go home with your cart still empty.

You return the next day with glue to set the figurines solidly in their places, a small box with "Donativo" written on it, and three new bags of gold, frankincense and myrrh.

♦ ♦ ♦

I love the meseta, and that is what I say when anyone says it's boring. "It's so flat." "It's just wheat fields." "There's no trees." Well, that's how it is when someone complains – they exaggerate.

After all, the first part of the meseta, west of Burgos, rolls like swells on the wide ocean. There are sunflower fields and charming small towns in narrow river valleys.

But there are not many trees, and on a hot afternoon, hikers long for shade. There have been valiant attempts at improving the situation. A few tree farms can be seen from the trail. Some hillsides are spiky with white plastic tubes supporting spindly saplings. Amazingly, the last fifty kilometers or so of the camino heading into León have been blessed by the hard work of whoever planted a continuous row of trees on the south side of the trail. I am curious about another section where trees line the north side of the path. My guess is that they were planted by a sympathetic landowner who, although unable to provide shade where peregrinos walk, at least wanted to contribute possible resting places out of the sun.

I wanted to do my part to make the meseta more lovable. So every day I ate an apple. The apples in Spain include varieties I've never eaten in North America, and they are delicious and crisp. I imagined apple trees providing shade and fruit to future peregrinos. So as I nibbled down to the core of each apple, I threw seeds into the disturbed dirt at the edge of fields to my left – the south side of the trail.

I know that growing apple trees from seed usually results in sour, possibly inedible, apples. I know it's likely that plows will go through and uproot potential sprouts.

But maybe a tree will grow and provide fruit, if not for human consumption, then for the birds. Maybe a tree will grow and provide shade and a resting place. If not, then at least my apple cores will have provided good composting material for a future garden of Eden.

THE JOKE CAMINO

Walking kilometer after kilometer on the camino, you finally get kilometers. Like other Americans, you know you've resisted the metric system only because you haven't used it day to day. With road signs, camino markers, the guidebook and your pilgrim passport all giving distances in kilometers, you don't even bother converting to miles anymore. You just know that with a backpack on, you walk about four kilometers per hour, twenty kilometers is a pretty easy day's walk, and thirty per day is about the maximum you'd want to do.

You used the metric system in high school science classes, of course. Somehow, it feels as though that's where metric belongs – in the lab. It is kind of a sterile system, everything being about tens, hundreds and thousands. You know the conversions are crazy in your system, things like 5,280 feet in a mile. But you like how feet relate to the length of human feet, how a mile is the approximate distance of a thousand double paces. You picture Roman soldiers counting Hut-one, Hut-two, Hut three up to Hut-one thousand as they marched, measuring

117

the miles of the expanding Roman Empire.

You walk with some British peregrinos, and you ask them about miles versus kilometers because their country converted to metric not that long ago. There are goods and bads to both systems, they concede. Like you, they found that the mile-to-kilometer transition was pretty easy. However, they definitely prefer the centigrade temperature scale. It just makes sense to have the freezing point at zero. Like walking kilometers to get used to them, you get dressed each morning and feel the heat or cold in relation to what the Celsius thermometer is telling you. It doesn't take too long to get good at it. You know they've got a point there, but on a warm day in Spain, when you look at a bank sign that flashes the time and the temperature, your initial instinct is to shudder when you read twenty-four degrees.

You have one more argument to raise. "The metric system doesn't have any romance to it," you say. They haven't heard of Robert Frost and "miles to go before I sleep." But when you start singing "500 kilometers, 500 kilometers, 500 kilometers, 500 kilometers, Lord I'm 500 kilometers from my home," slaughtering the smooth phrasing of the Peter, Paul and Mary song, they laugh and say, "Okay, okay, miles it is."

Now that you're not so intimidated by a foreign measuring system, you get curious, and you want to play with it. You know that the earth is 24,000 miles around the equator. That's 40,000 kilometers. There's a globe in one of the albergues where you stay between Santiago and Finisterre. You get a piece of string and figure out what portion of it equals 5,000 kilometers. You set one end of that segment at the west coast of Spain and voila! You had a feeling this would work! The other end of the 5,000 kilometer piece touches your home town on the coast of New England.

Two days later, you walk with a celebratory group of peregrinos from your albergue in Finisterre to the sandy beach on the other side of the peninsula. A few gather wood to build a big campfire on the sand. There's a tradition of burning boots or walking sticks or guidebooks or other peregrino paraphernalia here at the end of the earth. You've carried your worn out boots to the beach and toss them into the flames.

Someone has a guitar and, after quick consultation with the musician, you stand up and announce that you have a song you'd like to share, and that those who live on the east coast of North America will relate. You start to sing, "5,000 kilometers, 5,000 kilometers, 5,000 kilometers, 5,000 kilometers, Lord I'm 5,000 kilometers from my home," and everyone is singing, swaying, clapping, and laughing, especially watching you try to keep a straight face.

♦ TWO ♦

When your tongue is stumbling over foreign words, you might as well laugh about it, you figure. Sharing experiences with your fellow English-speaking pilgrims, you like to make your funny mistakes even funnier.

There's a Spanish peregrino you've seen along the way who's kind of a live wire. Even though you can't understand what he says, because he talks so fast, you like to listen to him. When he walks up to a group of his fellow countrymen-and-women on the trail he says, "Buen Camino" three times at warp speed.

You try it. It comes out "Blen melino, blen melino, blen melino." You try again. "Ben canino, ben canino, ben canino." Just getting through it without busting up is a feat.

Then there's the bicycle call you've made up. Frankly, you explain to your friends, you have a hard time with bicycles being on the same trail with hikers. There you are, humping along, concentrating to find good places to place your feet on rough trails, when one or more bikes come up from behind, sometimes with the sounding of a bell but sometimes silently. Back home if a bike comes up behind you, say on a bridge where bikes and pedestrians have to share the walkway, the bike rider will call out "On your right" or "On your left" so you immediately know which way to sidestep to let them pass without even having to turn around. Granted, on the camino, there are language barriers. There are four commonly heard languages — Spanish, French, German and English. So you get this idea and practice it in your head. The next time a bike comes up behind you without warning, you call out to hikers ahead of you, "Fahrrad, bicycle, bicicletta, velo" to give them a heads-up. They don't react at all. What? Are they Italians?

You try it a few more times, but with no success. Darn, you thought it was such a brilliant idea. So you switch to calling "Ding, ding" and that works. Everyone laughs, and the bike riders sail off over the next hill.

On an evening near the end of the hike, when everyone is relaxed and enjoying snacks and drinks at a cluster of sidewalk tables, your favorite Spanish tongue twister is born.

There's one guy from Canada who, even after weeks of hiking, says "pelegrino" instead of "peregrino" for pilgrim. Either his ear just wants the "l" in there to make it more like the English word or maybe, at home, he drinks the mineral water of that name. You caution him, though, about the possible confusion with the word you've seen on signs at construction sites. "Peligroso" means dangerous.

At that, another person at the table pulls out a Spanish-English dictionary and opens to the "pel-" to "per-" page, and the word "perezoso" catches her eye. "Lazy," she translates for us.

"Okay, say 'lazy dangerous pilgrim' in Spanish three times fast," you challenge, and everyone starts muttering "Perezoso peligroso peregrino," even though that isn't the correct construction in Spanish where adjectives usually come after the noun. No one can do it fast, and hardly anyone gets it correct. But the truly funny part comes when people start trying to figure out what a lazy dangerous pilgrim could possibly be, and what kinds of crazy things you could do to qualify as one.

◆ THREE ◆

You and your three best friends have an interesting set of traits in common. You all like to be active – you've done a bike relay as a team every summer for the past eight years. You're professional women in competitive fields so you're all hard-headed and outspoken. And you read advice columnists because you consider them to be pretty smart cookies, and you like it when their opinions back up your own.

The camino is the longest and most challenging trip you've done together, and you're only in Estella so there's a long way to go yet. The four-way hard-headedness is getting to you. Do there have to be differences of opinion about everything? About which route to take when there are choices? About when to stop for coffee? About sitting at a table in the sun or the shade? About what time to start out in the morning? You're all tired, so the stating of personal preferences is beginning to sound like whining.

You need to take action before you explode. So the next time the yammer-yammer starts up, you throw up your hands and blurt, "Dear Abby, my three best friends are driving me crazy." They all stop and look at you.

"It isn't Abby anymore. It's her daughter or the other one's

daughter.”

“There's Dear Caroline, too. And Miss Manners.”

“Whatever,” you say. “It can be Señorita Smarty-Pants for all I care. What would she say about us?”

They look at each other. One asks, “Is that the whole letter or do you want to add some detail?”

You stick out your lower lip. “That's it for now.”

The second says, “Well, you know, one thing I like about Señorita Smarty-Pants is that she has a balanced point of view. It's never all the fault of one party or the other. So she might ask everyone, including the writer of the letter, to consider her part in creating the craziness.”

The next says “I think she would suggest being specific instead of using the words ‘driving me crazy.’ She'd advise you to be clear with your friends about how and where you want them to drive you if not to crazy-land.”

Yeah, yeah, yammer-yammer, you think, staring at the ground.

Then the first one speaks up again. “The Señorita might just say, ‘Focus on the first four words rather than the last four.’” You look up at her blankly. So she adds in her best Spanish accent, “The phrase ’My three best friends’ holds much more weight in my advice column than the words ‘are driving me crazy’.”

Then your friend does one of those loud high-pitched Aye-yi-yi-yi-yi-yi things for good measure. You all dissolve into laughter, but your eyes seem to be the only ones that tear up and threaten to overflow. So, quickly you put your arms around all three of them and say, “I love you guys,” and you hold on for a good long while.

For the rest of the camino, through Lagroño, Burgos, León, Astorga, Ponferrada, O Cebreiro, Sarria, Mélide, and into Santiago, whenever the going gets tough, you and your three tough friends call on Señorita Smarty-Pants for advice and, no surprise, she gets cheekier and saucier all the time. Aye-yi-yi-yi-yi-yi!

♦ ♦ ♦

The most charming albergue my husband and I stayed in was in Santa Mariña, one long day's walk before reaching the coast of Spain. The albergue was a small stone house with a flagstone patio in back and farm fields beyond. When we approached the door, another peregrino staying there told us the landlady would be back soon and had left instructions that any other arrivals should go ahead and make themselves at home.

We left our boots by the back door and padded past the kitchen, the downstairs bedroom with just two sets of bunk beds in it, through the sitting room and up the stairs to a charming space lit by skylights, complete with six single beds and a small bathroom under slanted ceilings. After cleaning up, I headed immediately back down the stairs to the sitting room which was furnished with a love seat, cushioned chairs, and what to me was the main attraction -- floor-to-ceiling shelves stuffed full of books in different languages. I was in heaven.

I'd been suffering from reading withdrawal all through the trip. At home, I always have a book on the go and probably read an average of a book a week. On the camino, I didn't want to carry the extra weight, and most others were the same. The only two peregrinos I saw reading had picked up books left behind at albergues, and one of those was Dumas' The Three Musketeers with the first two hundred and last hundred pages missing. The reader reasoned that he could still enjoy the style if not the story.

As I poured over the titles of the books at the albergue in Santa Mariña, I pictured the landlady as a slim cosmopolitan middle-aged well-educated woman with an artistic bent. She still had not returned from wherever she had gone, but I looked forward to meeting her. In the meantime, I had some laundry to do.

The other resident peregrino had mentioned a laundry sink, but I'd looked everywhere and hadn't seen it. I'd gone up and down the stairs twice to double check myself. So I proceeded to do laundry in the large kitchen sink.

That's when the landlady showed up, as I had a pile of freshly washed and wrung out undies and socks on the drain board, a couple of shirts in the soapy water, and a pair of pants at my feet. She was short, round, old and half-bald, and when she saw what I was doing, she proceeded to call on all the saints for help. She shook her head, setting her jowls awobble, crossed herself repeatedly and cried "¡Dios mío, Dios mío!"

"Lo siento," I said. I'm sorry. And I tried to explain in my limited Spanish that I couldn't find the laundry sink. She stormed out, throwing up her hands in exasperation.

I guiltily finished washing my clothes, hung them on the line to dry, then took another look around the house. Oh, there was the utility sink, tucked under the stairs, just opposite the sitting room. Every time I'd passed there previously, my eyes had been drawn to the books, and I'd totally missed that little cubbyhole.

Anyway, she forgave me when we went next door to register and pay and was happy that we'd be eating dinner in her bar. The funny thing was that in addition to not matching my fantasy landlady in appearance, this seventy-six year old woman, the owner of a lovely house full of good reading material, either had bad eyes or was barely literate. Her granddaughter handled all of the registration and made sure her grandma held the pilgrim passport stamp right-side-up.

I committed one more laundry sin along the camino. Back in Santiago again after having walked to Finisterre, my husband and I stayed at a small and pleasant pensión. It was a Sunday and laundries were closed, so again I did washing in a sink. I hung shirts and pants close to the open windows of our room to dry.

We came back to our lodgings later, after a walk around town. The landlady, quite upset, was explaining that she had had to move the hanging clothes somewhere else to dry and something about "policía." I guess Santiago de Compostela has bylaws about not hanging laundry in public view. Who knew?

I murmured my Spanish apologies again. Then when we'd gone upstairs to our room and had the door firmly shut behind us, I turned to my husband, crossed myself repeatedly and warbled, "¡Dios mío, Dios mío!"

THE MEDITATION CAMINO

♦ ONE ♦

You turn sixty-three while you're walking the camino. Other peregrinos you've met, who are about your age, have just retired and that's why they're doing the camino now. Not you. You're at the top of your game. You own a successful company with over one hundred employees, and you jet around doing business internationally. You take a week off every month and a month off every year. You've traveled a lot and you like adventure travel – biking across countries, climbing mountains, paddling remote rivers, heli-skiing, stuff like that.

Hiking the camino fits into this category, especially the way you're doing it – thirty-five to forty kilometers per day and no days off. You laugh when you call it the Type A approach. A couple of your business buddies did it last year and didn't talk at all afterward about what they'd seen along the way, only about how many days it took them to complete the trip. You thought, I bet I can do it faster.

Now it looks as though you've succeeded. You stayed in Palas de Rei last night with only seventy-three kilometers to go. You can finish tomorrow, and that puts your total number of days at two less than your friends'. You know they'll be impressed.

When you see the sixty-three kilometer marker on the edge of Leboreiro, you ask another peregrino to take a picture of you. You pose, pointing with one thumb at the number sixty-three on the marker and pointing with the other thumb at yourself. This gives you an idea. You'll remember highlights from each year of your life as the numbers go down between here and Santiago.

Okay, sixty-three is easy. You have twelve days' worth of memories to reflect on for one kilometer. Sixty-two is easy, too. Last year is still clear as a bell. But then as you pass the sixty-one and sixty markers, you realize you're not exactly sure in which year certain things happened, so you decide instead to consider five-year blocks of time over five kilometers, a little over an hour, of walking.

What a difference that makes! It's like your brain kicked into a lower gear, and instead of spinning crazily, it is working in smooth steady circles, drawing in associations and sensory recall and layers of emotion with something like centripetal force.

Between the sixty and fifty-five markers, you think about your parents' deaths and how you were suddenly the oldest member of your family, how your own mortality loomed before you. Between fifty-five and fifty, you think about your second marriage, what makes it different from the first and in what ways it is the same, indicating that you still have things you're supposed to learn. Between fifty and forty, breakthroughs in your work come to mind, but so do fishing trips and learning to surf.

You are coming into Arzúa and see in your guidebook that ahead is one of those rare twenty kilometer stretches of the camino where there are no accommodations. You are at kilometer forty-two, so a long day tomorrow will still get you into Santiago. Meanwhile, you have to admit it feels good to finish earlier than usual. You sit outside an ice cream shop across the street from the plaza and get a kick out of the statue on the square of a brother and sister working at cross purposes in handling a pair of calves. You look forward to tomorrow morning's walk when, between the forty and thirty kilometer markers, two hours will be devoted to memories of your own children, when they were a boy and girl at odds like the two in the sculpture.

After a great night's sleep filled with dreams, you continue down the trail and down the years. You alternately chuckle and sigh, remembering the decade of coexisting with young children.

Your walk from the thirty marker to the twenty is about the romance of being young, being smart and handsome, being a business hotshot, and being in love with your first wife. At kilometer twenty-four you find yourself in the lovely small crossroads town of Santa Irene, a town that shares your first wife's name, Irene, and who you married at age twenty-four. That's pretty surreal.

As you begin the final twenty kilometers into Santiago, you sense the edges of your remembered-self going fuzzy. The memories are more fluid, more communal, more timeless and suspended – like images of the high school dance where, instead of pairing off into self-conscious couples, everyone danced in a big circle; like when your family went camping and watched sparks from the fire fly upward toward the stars, and everyone made up stories about new constellations that were forming; like the summer you and your friend collected periwinkle shells on the beach and glued them into designs on pieces of scrap lumber and felt like real artists; like when you lay on the floor under your grandfather's grand piano listening to him play Broadway tunes and wiggling your fingers along.

The kilometer markers must have run out somewhere around twelve or thirteen. You're pretty sure that one of those was the last you saw. You weren't paying attention, so completely were you inhabiting another time.

But here's Monte do Gozo, one of the places where probably every peregrino stops for at least a short break. Monte do Gozo translates as Mount of Highest Pleasure. Historically, it is from this point, five kilometers from the city, that pilgrims tried to catch a first glimpse of the spires of the great cathedral. It was a bit of a competition. The first one, in a group of pilgrims, to spot them would be proclaimed the pilgrim king.

You can't see them. The city is hazed in and there's a lot of new construction. You look instead at the huge monument to Pope John Paul II's pilgrimages in 1982 and 1989 that sits atop this hill. It's kind of monstrous. You then go into the bustling café, realize how hungry you are and order a meal, something you don't usually do until you're done walking for the day.

Then you surprise yourself. You decide this is the end of your day, and you get a hotel room in the big holiday complex here. You'll only beat out your buddies by one day instead of two. Who cares? You don't anymore. More important to you, at the moment, is that you have no memories of the time before you were five, and you don't know what you'll think about as you walk tomorrow. It worries you, because remembering has become your mission on the camino, a mission you feel you must complete as surely as you finish the hike itself.

In the morning you still have no insights and start your walk with your head down and a scowl on your face. But as you warm up and enjoy the cool air on your skin and the light and shadow on the path and the sense of anticipation among those you pass or who pass you, you forget your worries. You look around like, well yes, like a kid, and you realize you are seeing more than you have the whole rest of the trip. You become a creature of sensation, empty of thought, full of curiosity.

It feels like more than five kilometers as the suburban sidewalks stretch on, and you wonder if the five kilometer measurement was maybe from Monte do Gozo to just the edge of the city of Santiago de Compostela. From the outskirts to the cathedral, then, your remembering will have to go prenatal. So in your imagination you tuck yourself into a perfect warm and safe place.

When you reach the main plaza in front of the church, you hardly recognize yourself. You hesitate to use the word "reborn" but there it is. A paradise has been inside you all this time, and it only took sixty-three kilometers of walking to unearth it.

♦ TWO ♦

You care so much about the well-being of the planet that it hurts. At home, when you grow your urban veggie garden, go to the recycling center, take public transportation, install a solar water heater in your condo, shop for groceries, shop for anything, you're aware of the environmental impacts of the choices you are making.

But it's not just a mind thing. This is true love. You get it that the earth is your mother, the source of life.

You go to work four days a week and make a decent income. You give as much as you can afford to the Sierra Club, the Nature Conservancy, Greenpeace and lots of smaller organizations besides. You feel like you want to do even more, but what else is there?

You're finding out while you walk the camino. You thought that by traveling across an ocean and putting on a backpack, you were escaping your normal cares. You didn't expect this hike to be part of your save-the-world program. But you sense that something significant is happening here, that some healing of the planet is resulting from you and all these peregrinos tromping across Spain.

In the past year, everywhere you've turned there has been information about noetic science. It's even in the latest Dan Brown thriller that you read on the plane on the way over to Europe. The idea is that thoughts are energy, and the more people who are thinking about, visualizing, or praying for something, the more energy that is set in motion to, potentially, make that something happen.

Here on the camino, more than 100,000 people walk each year, noticing the beauty and bounty of the land. Just as children thrive when they are noticed and appreciated, so too does the earth. You know this for sure, although you can't explain how you know. Maybe a noetic scientist could help you in this regard. Over the centuries, all of the sciences have added new vocabulary to languages, giving shape to concepts that, at first, seemed wild and outrageous but that came to be seen as acceptable and even ordinary.

You've always sensed things that couldn't be seen, heard, smelled or touched. You think it's too bad that the term "extra-sensory perception" has come to be associated with reading minds. You'd like it to mean simply what it says – perceiving outside the usual five senses. You get messages, either verbal or emotional, from nature, from relationship patterns and systems that are out of balance, from people who have died. You feel bombarded with messages along the camino – messages about healing and community and the flow of life toward death. But do those messages come through your skin, eyes, ears, nose, or tongue? Yes. No.

The camino is affecting you in a very deep way. It feels molecular.

You have to remind yourself every once in a while that there is another reality. You make yourself apply logic to the question of how these messages will manifest in everyday life.

You have to admit that between going to work, travelling via public transportation, taking care of your garden, and contributing time and money to good causes, you don't do much else. Your money talks, but do you walk the talk?

At the moment you are, literally, and that is making a huge difference in how you think about contributing to good causes. By walking the camino, across the red earth and green hills of the east, the wide plain of the center, the fragrant forests of the west, you're embodying a prayer. The prayer is very powerful, because of the energy of 100,000 people joining in. And now you get it. You can walk in this manner anywhere and at any time.

This is the something more that you can do to help save Planet Earth. You can walk on it, appreciating the beauty and bounty. You can visualize healthy webs of living things in every clump of bushes, every stand of trees, every field of grasses. You can walk to get places or to go nowhere particular. You can thank the land you walk upon. You can invite your friends to join you. You realize that we're all peregrinos, wherever we are and whether we know it or not.

♦ THREE ♦

In your real life, you're the retail manager of an outdoor equipment store. You train employees to handle stock, handle money, and handle customers. You know that friendly service is the key to a successful business, so you instill in those who work for you the importance of smiling and being pleasant. You have them role-play customer service situations saying "How may I help you?" instead of "May I help you?" You ask them to give what you call value-added service, where one extra bit of helpful information is offered in addition to the straightforward answer to a customer question. You have them practice giving clear directions for how to find things. And you discuss the importance of paying attention to body language, one's own as well as that of members of the public.

Modeling being patient and upbeat on the job drains you. Every year, you take three weeks to go as far away as you can to recharge your batteries. Sometimes you go to the beach, sometimes to the mountains. You usually feel refreshed for about a week after you get back from vacation. Then it's back to the same old, same old.

Your best friend asked you to hike the camino with her this year. Your first reaction was that this would drain your batteries further rather than recharge them, but she insisted it would be great. Ah well, it would give you first-hand experience with some of the new backpacking and hiking equipment in the store. You'd be able to praise the comfort of the latest hiking socks and the stress-reducing qualities of the new trekking poles. Sheeesh. Business.

The two of you fly to Madrid and take the train to León to begin walking. Three-hundred kilometers in three weeks should at least give you something else to think about besides shop issues.

You quickly discover that walking the camino isn't just a distraction; it's a whole way of life with its own rituals, social customs, culture and languages. You feel as though you've been adopted into a very large and loving family that trusts you'll make a smooth transition to being a peregrino without dwelling on, or perseverating about, your other life.

The camino family includes others besides just pilgrims. The locals too are genuinely friendly and welcoming even though they must feel overwhelmed at times by having so many people traipsing through their towns and filling up their coffee shops and yakking at them in any number of languages.

You are impressed by the helpful service you receive in shops, even though your Spanish is minimal and your pronunciation far from perfect. You've never felt that anyone got impatient with you or questioned your intelligence just because you speak Spanish baby talk. You ask yourself if you can make the same claim for yourself and your sales crew when it comes to waiting on customers who are less than fluent in English.

There's something else about the locals, and you're not sure if you're reading the signals correctly, but here is your guess. You and other peregrinos always say "Hola" or "Buen Camino" in passing each other, but you don't know the expectations about addressing those who live here. So your customer contact instincts kick in and you smile, make eye contact, and say "Buenos dias" to business owners standing outside their shops, people walking their dogs in parks, ladies leaning over their balcony railings, couples on park benches, farmers in their fields, old folks on their way to Mass, joggers, bikers and wheelchair pushers. You instantly notice body language, just as you do on the job, and this is so cool. Their heads pop up, tilted a little to the side, their eyes widen and the corners of their mouths lift just a bit. They greet you in return and their heads nod a few times, as if acknowledging a blessing that has just been bestowed upon them.

You ask your friend if she knows anything about it being considered good luck to be greeted by a pilgrim. She hasn't heard anything. You want to say hello to more people on the street, just to see that little spark of happiness on their faces. You decide that, whether or not your greeting is interpreted as a blessing by them, you are going to speak it with that intention.

You feel your batteries recharging day after day, "Hola" after "Hola."

There is nothing pretend about your smile now. Why on earth had you been referring to work as real life? This is what's real, you decide – the giving and receiving of blessings. You try to imagine how you will present this new approach to your staff. Will they think you've gone completely bonkers?

♦ ♦ ♦

I'm a failed meditator. In the 70s, when I heard about Transcendental Meditation, a.k.a. TM, I went to the introductory session and was given a personal mantra. My practice lasted, maybe, two weeks and that was with several attempts at changing the mantra to something that was more pleasing to my ear.

For a few years, in the 80s, I was part of a shamanic drumming circle, but as soon as I moved away from that city and the supportive community that shared that interest with me, drumming and shamanic journeying got dropped.

I've been to a few Buddhist meditation sessions and have read books about the practice. I've always said I should make time for daily meditation, but it hasn't happened yet.

One of my friends said to me, "Your whole life is a meditation," and that made me feel better. But I realized I didn't know exactly what she meant by that. Maybe she was referring to my not having a television or other media technology. Maybe she was thinking about how I spend lots of time alone. Maybe she was wondering what else I could be doing during my long-distance drives considering that I never turn on the radio in the car.

When I first heard the term "walking meditation," something clicked. I could totally relate to that idea.

Regular walking is something I've done since I was a teenager. It got me through the emotional angst of adolescence, through the early years of motherhood and the temporary evaporation of my adult brain, through relationship melt-downs and lonely times.

In the physical realm, it has kept me feeling healthy and fit. And in the artistic, I've discovered that getting stuck during the creative process is fixed by going for a walk. Movement helps the brain synthesize, and brilliant solutions seem to pop out of nowhere.

I learned a walking meditation technique at a retreat one summer. The members of the group were instructed to think of a situation or problem for which a solution was sought. A clear question was to be formulated before the walk started. Then as we entered the forest trail system, we were to put our questions out to the natural world that surrounded us. We walked then, waiting, watching, listening, and sure enough answers came.

I knew that walking the camino would be a meditation, but I didn't realize what a difference it would make to do it hour after hour, day after day, as compared with just a weekend retreat. Problems, questions, and even answers were completely blown out of my head by the deep breaths needed for getting up steep hills, sweated out by the warmth of the Mediterranean sun and the heat of exertion, aroma-therapied out by the smells of pine, honeysuckle, mown grass and eucalyptus, drummed out by the rhythmic pounding of feet and walking sticks, flushed out by the liters of water drunk every day, and tickled out by all the little wonders that made me laugh.

No problems, no questions, no answers? No, and not much thinking either. A spacious emptiness filled the inside of my skull like the inside of a pale blue balloon. So that's what meditators go for, I thought. That emptiness made it possible for me to not be reactive, to not get upset by little things, to not take other people's crankiness personally, to not feel like I had to be Ms. Fix-It at signs of trouble. What a relief!

I talked with other peregrinos about this, about the empty brain feeling and also about an image I had of being an atom of water in a big river, flowing along with all the other atoms. They nodded their heads and said, Yes, they'd felt that, too.

I found that if conversations steered toward the distant past, the distant future, or distant lands, I couldn't go there. "Let's stay on the camino," I'd suggest, hearing echoes of Ram Dass in the 70s saying "Be here now."

Walking the camino changed me. I say that unequivocally. But you know what? I don't want to analyze it or question it or attach words to how that change feels. I just want to sit with it and watch it move in and out with my breath. Come to think of it, those are words used by meditation teachers. Maybe I've finally figured out how it works.

THE ART CAMINO

♦ ONE ♦

You love the name of this mountain between Pamplona and Puente la Reina. Alto del Perdón — The Hill of Forgiveness. But why would there be talk of forgiveness here when it's still 680 kilometers to Santiago de Compostela where, belief has it, all of a pilgrim's sins will be forgiven? You're sure there's an old story to explain the name, but you haven't seen any reference to one. So as you walk, you make one up.

In the early 1500s, you postulate, a group of pilgrims was travelling to Santiago. They had come together as strangers at the Tour Saint-Jacques in Paris. It was common knowledge that there was safety in numbers on the Camino de Santiago, where robbers and charlatans lay in wait for the unsuspecting and the unprotected.

They'd been travelling for almost two months and were halfway to their goal. Two months was long enough, in such close proximity, that they now felt they knew each other too well. Bickering had escalated into yelling matches. Suspicion of each other's honesty had almost overshadowed concern about thievery on the trail. Shifting alliances and jealousies had everyone feeling vulnerable and hurt.

The fog was thick as they climbed this hill, and each pilgrim could barely see the hem of the cape of the person ahead. It was eerie walking blindly, and more than one of them thought that the centuries-long war against the Moors, which had ended only decades ago, had obliterated the landscape. They found themselves listening for the familiar sounds of each other – the creaky boots, the rumbling burps, the animals' nickers, the wheezing breaths. Occasionally, one member of the group or another couldn't help but nervously call out the name of someone whom they could neither hear nor see in the mist and would be answered with a gruff "Harrumph."

When their feet finally found level ground at the top, they stopped as one to catch their breath. At that moment, the fog started to lift as though their exhalations were pushing the grayness away. The green and gold valley below, the red roofs of the villages, the blue cliffs of the Cordillera Cantábrica in the distance and, finally, their own brown wool cloaks were illuminated like a picture in a holy book. The sun touched them like a brush of gold paint, and they felt the divine nature of each other's presence. Forgiveness was offered and received without a word being spoken, and the men and women took a moment to smile or nod to each other before setting off west once more.

You reach the top of the hill having enjoyed splendid views the whole way up and, to your utter amazement, there stands the band of pilgrims from your story. Along the edge of the plateau is a line of eleven life-size pilgrims cut from flat metal and weathered to various shades of rust. Two ride horses, one rides a donkey, and one leads a mule. The others walk, leaning into the gentle wind that blew the fog away in your story, and their cloaks, kerchiefs and hair stream behind. In their hands are long walking sticks, and from the tops, odd bits of metal seem to flutter like prayers of thankfulness and sighs of relief.

You take off your pack and sit leaning against it as you drink the two cans of cold pop you've bought out of the back of an enterprising local's truck. You get a kick out of watching the negative space between the metal pilgrims' bodies get filled in and layered by the shapes of today's live pilgrims who are meandering, talking, pointing and taking pictures in front of the sculpture. Windmills spin on other peaks of the Sierra del Perdón. A peregrino with a deep resonant voice starts singing Johnny Cash tunes, and others join in for a line or two. The sun touches the whole scene with a brush of gold.

◆ TWO ◆

Whenever you've traveled, you've always gone into old churches. You love stone and stained glass and arches and lofty ceilings. But you know very little about architecture. To you, a cathedral is a cathedral is a cathedral.

When you previewed the Camino de Santiago guidebook before leaving home, you read that the Catedral de Santa María in Burgos and the Catedral de León are impressive examples of Gothic architecture, and the Real Basílica de San Isidoro in León is a seminal work in the Romanesque style. The Catedral del Apóstol in Santiago is also Romanesque, but the famous western face has a lavish baroque façade that was added in the 18th century.

You pulled out the A volume of an old authoritative encyclopedia and looked up "architecture." All of a sudden, your brain started making connections between words like nave and apse, arch and vault, pier and flying buttress and memories of features you'd seen as a tourist. You were certain that knowing the terminology would help you see the details that earned those Spanish cathedrals their status as world-class examples of architectural styles.

Now, as you hike each day, you find yourself doing something you've never done before in your travels — you're making drawings in your journal. When you see a particularly majestic or unusual church building, and that happens several times a day, you take a few minutes' break there, pull out your notebook and pen, and recreate the shapes and contours you see before you. Your grade eight art unit on how to draw perspective is coming back to you.

Sometimes you draw columns and rounded arches and solid sturdy walls and label them "Romanesque." These churches were built in the 11th and 12th centuries, and even though that was six or seven hundred years after the fall of the Roman Empire, it's still easy for you to see the "Roman" in "Romanesque."

Your drawing skills get tested as you sketch in front of Gothic cathedrals that were built between 1200 and 1500 — all those upward pointing arches and upward pointing spires and flying buttresses that, from beyond the outer walls of the building, provide lateral support for those amazingly high upward pointed ceilings. And then there are wild-faced gargoyles and spiky spiny protuberances! You've heard that the motivation for the Gothic style was to draw the eye up toward heaven, but you can't help feeling that there was a blatant demonstration of earthly political and ecclesiastical power going on as well.

By the time you reach Santiago, your journal is full of pictures and notes and the kinds of questions that having just a little bit of knowledge tend to spark. But you've saved the last page for drawing the Catedral del Apóstol.

You sit on a bench in the plaza and first draw the hefty square shapes and the main columns and arches that were constructed starting in 1075. Then you take a breath and decide to just let your pen go wild to add the baroque curlicues that remind you of drips and swirls of frosting on a fancy cake.

You realize now why you couldn't make heads or tails out of architecture before. When it took centuries to build huge cathedrals after which additions and facelifts and façades were added, the styles got all jumbled up. You think of all the individuals who must have hoped to make personal statements with their contributions to the stonework, the stained glass, the arches and ribs and bell towers that reached for the sky. You leaf through your journal and see that those individual statements combine to create quite an architectural conversation. You're pleased that you've caught a few snippets of it along the camino and that, this time, you actually understood some of what you heard.

♦ THREE ♦

You are a historian, and you take great pleasure in research. You are also a believer and take equal pleasure in turning off your analytical mind to find a different kind of truth.

This is why you really appreciate art. When it's doing its job, it combines what the head knows and what the heart knows, so it makes you think as well as feel.

When you look at historical art, as you are certainly doing along the camino, there's a third kind of knowing that occurs to you – sort of a group-mind kind of truth. You try to figure it out as you look at the statue of El Cid in Burgos.

He sits on the back of his powerful horse, larger than life, sword raised and dressed for battle, in the middle of a traffic circle, seeming to challenge the modern armored attackers who have him surrounded and buzz like annoying insects. El Cid, a national hero for taking back

142

the city of Valencia from the Moors in 1094, was born Rodrigo Diaz in 1043 just north of Burgos.

In 1064, he was a pilgrim on the Camino de Santiago, but your analytical mind tells you that did not make him a godly man. For in the next thirty years, he was to fight for any ruler, Christian or Muslim, as long as his own personal power and fortune benefited. In other words, he was a mercenary.

Your heart knows that he was very brave, and he had guts. You can see those qualities in the statue by the way he's portrayed sitting on the horse, by the way he holds his head.

The third kind of knowing that you are exploring here has to do with the fact that until the Renaissance, art's purpose was not to express the interior life and thoughts of the artist but to express the needs and desires of a people or their rulers. The artist had to be sensitive to what was being said, what was being left unsaid, and who was doing the talking.

The Muslims had started invading Spain from the south in the early 700s and had, within decades, overrun most of the country. Economically, educationally, and artistically this brought many benefits to Spain. But when the grave of St. James was discovered in Santiago in 813, the Christian population felt inspired to intensify their resistance to the Moors and to reclaim what was theirs. At the time of El Cid, 250 years later, the fight was still going on and had a long way to go. Spain needed a hero, and poets and artists heard that need and put El Cid up on a pedestal.

The other war hero in this long struggle against the Moors was someone who had died centuries before in the year 44. Yes, St. James, Santiago himself, supposedly jumped into the fray.

Artists had heard the need. The Spanish were despondent, believing that the Moors were unstoppable because they carried with them the arm bone of their prophet Mohammed. Well then, since the bones of Santiago had been found in Galicia, surely St. James could come to the aid of the Christian armies. Painters and sculptors portrayed him doing just that.

You visit the Museo de las Peregrinaciones in Santiago de Compostela at the end of your hike. Admission is free for pilgrims. One whole gallery is devoted to images of St. James and there he is, in several paintings and sculptures, looking somewhat like the warrior El Cid with his cape flying and sword raised, sitting on the back of a mighty white steed. Christian soldiers actually saw Santiago leading them into battle, killing Muslims left and right, earning him the title "Matamoros," the Moor Slayer.

Your head tells you this: that the soldiers had probably prayed fervently to St. James before the battle, then approached the enemy with a severe calorie deficit, racing hearts, fast breathing, and chanting the name of Santiago. No wonder they saw him. Conditions were ripe for hallucination.

Your heart tells you that miracles do happen, not to the extent that dead men lead armies, but in the sense that prayer and belief can make the difference between winning and losing.

Thinking about the third kind of truth requires that you be sensitive to the relationship between St. James and Spain. As an apostle, James supposedly brought Christ's teachings to the Iberian peninsula. After he was beheaded in Jerusalem, becoming the first Christian martyr, it is said that his body was carried by boat to the shores of Spain by two of his followers and buried inland at the site of what is now Santiago de Compostela. Santiago is the patron saint of the country. There is a deep love for him here, and the Spanish outnumber any other nationality among peregrinos on the camino.

It turns out you also have a strong connection to him, and during your walk on the camino, it started to feel like love. Your middle name is James, chosen by your parents because it is a saint's name, this saint. You've hiked the camino as a historian, as a believer, as a lover of art, and as a James. You look carefully at the images in the gallery, asking yourself which is your favorite, which one could be a hero now in the 21st century. You select a small figurine, set into a niche. This artist's rendition shows a quiet, intelligent and calmly charismatic figure -- just what today's world needs, you think.

◆ ◆ ◆

Sometimes pieces of art grab me and won't let me go. It first happened when I was in college in West Virginia and found an out-of-the-way area of the library in which to study. The art folio books were on a shelf right behind me, and for breaks I would reach for one. I had had no previous exposure to great works of art, so this was an act not just of opening books but of opening worlds. Monet and Klimt grabbed me for sure, and I found it impossible to get back to studying for at least a half hour once I'd lost myself in the worlds they created with paint.

The next time it happened, I was visiting the Museum of Modern Art in New York City. There was a portrait of a girl in one of the huge galleries, and even though I started to walk away from it three times, I had to retrace those steps and look at it again. I sat on the bench in front of her trying to figure out why this particular painting was demanding my attention. It wasn't anything about the technique or the style or the colors. The only thing I could come up with that might explain the strength of my attraction was that I must have been that girl in a previous life. It was that gripping.

Walking the camino was like strolling through a very long and linear gallery. Every small village, medium-sized town and big city had at least one beautiful church that drew me in for a look, just like the folios had drawn me in during my college days.

Also, there were statues of peregrinos all along the way, some on town squares, some on hilltops, some in the seeming middle of nowhere. Each had one foot in front of the other, a simple but effective psychological boost to those of us walking by. My favorites reflect the delightful diversity of the works to be seen. In the square in Santo Domingo was a statue where the pilgrim himself was invisible. There, in worked metal, were all the trappings of a peregrino – a bicycle, a tall hooked walking stick with calabash and scallop shell attached, a hat, rumpled backpack and boot – arranged in such a way that a traveler could be imagined in the empty spaces between objects.

In Burgos, just beyond one of the gates of the old town, stands the very solid representation of a male pilgrim in a full-length cape, wide-brimmed hat and tall walking stick, and beside him a woman in an old-fashioned dress but no traveling clothes. They are both nearly as wide as they are tall and have big smiles on their faces. When I look at the photo I took of them, it makes me think he is happy to be going and she is happy to be rid of him.

On a hilltop in Galicia, where the wind blows continually up from a valley to the south, an eight-foot-tall bronze pilgrim leans his head far to the left and has his hand firmly on top of it to keep his hat from blowing off. Passing pilgrims take the same pose in front of the statue and take turns snapping photos of each other.

There was one work of art along the camino that truly grabbed me, and I wonder to this day about its story. The sculpture stands in Negreira, west of Santiago de Compostela, so I'm not even sure it's about pilgrimage.

As my husband and I walked toward it along the road from our previous night's lodging, we saw the ragged section of stone wall implying a house, a boy leaning out a window and grasping the pant leg of a man, his father, who is just about to walk away carrying a knapsack over his shoulder. There is a look on the man's face of despair. Or is it determination? Or both?

"Are his leg's turning into tree trunks?" I asked as we drew nearer.

"Sure looks like it," my husband said. "Either that or he's literally pulling up roots."

I speculated that there might be an old folk tale about a boy whose love for his father kept the man from being able to leave home. Was there a reference here to the Spanish Civil War? Or the statue could be telling the relatively modern story of families being torn apart by the economic necessity for emigration. Then I walked around to a place where I could see the rear of the sculpture.

"The plot thickens," I said.

Sitting on a chair with her back to the wall is a woman, the mother I assume. She is holding a baby and looking towards what is happening between father and son. Her expression is sorrowful and helpless. What will she do, I wondered?

When I got home, I looked online for information, for the story about this work of art, but all I found were mentions of it in peregrino blogs. They described it as a cool statue. They didn't say one word about the sad woman behind the wall.

THE SOCIAL CAMINO

♦ ONE ♦

You have a girlfriend at home. That's been a good thing in your life since the day you met her at university three years ago. But now that you're two weeks into walking the camino, an adventure she made very clear was of no interest to her, the good thing feels complicated.

There are lots of young people hiking. The camino seems to be the international thing-to-do between graduation and the start of a career. Some people use the walking time to figure out what they want to do with their lives. The conversations among 20-somethings pick up easily and get very intense and very personal, especially if there are bottles of wine going around.

You know what you are going to do with your life. You're going into medicine. You notice that some of the guys your age who are talking about working in their uncle's construction business for a year or doing more traveling shrug off that piece of information. But the girls light up picturing you as a doctor in a clean white lab coat. They touch your arm when they talk to you and give you hugs when they run into you again after not seeing you for two or three days.

Loyalty is messing with your emotions. Lately, after checking in at an albergue, you've been going off by yourself instead of hanging out with others in the kitchen or on the patio. You're trying to avoid the temptation to flirt back with attractive women who have this amazing camino experience in common with you. You go outside and check out what there is of a town and sometimes end up sitting by yourself on the steps of a church. Loneliness fills you up then, like dark floodwater, and you watch couples and families in the plaza and almost feel like crying.

You think a lot about just going home. It would be easier that way. You and your girlfriend would make wedding arrangements. After the marriage, you'd go to Greece for your honeymoon. Then she'd work in the accounting office while you continued your medical training. That's what you've planned. That's what you've envisioned.

But that picture looks dull from this angle. You feel so alive here. It's like everything you've seen and everyone you've met is glowing. What interesting people peregrinos are! They all seem so open to whatever comes their way. Walking the camino is not about having a plan, it's about being part of the flow of life. But if you give yourself free rein, if you go with the flow, you might put your relationship at risk.

You're sitting on the steps of a church once again, and you turn on your cell phone. There's a message from your girlfriend. You call back and, with your forehead on your hand, you listen to all her news about what's going on at home. When she says she misses you and asks when you'll be home, you feel a jolt. You find yourself reaching into your vest pocket to pull out your pilgrim passport that tells how many kilometers it is between towns all the way to Santiago. You leaf through the pages. "Hello?" she says.

"Let's see," you say, and you tell her how far you have come and how far you have left to go. You do some figuring out loud about the number of kilometers you do per day and how many more rest days you'll need. You give what you realize is a ridiculous range of dates for when she might be able to expect you. She sighs, and you know her eyes are going glassy. You laugh and kiss into the phone and say an abrupt goodbye. Then you stand and, with a catch in your breath and a shy smile, wave to some girls you know who are sitting outside the café across the square.

◆ TWO ◆

Five days into your camino, a pair of great legs passes you on the trail. They're long and strong. "Hola. Buen Camino," you say, and he says "Hola" back.

He's at the same albergue in Puente la Reina as you are that evening, and you've both bought groceries for dinner. You nod to each other, and you ask in English with welcoming gestures if he'd like to eat with you. He answers in Danish and says your accent gave you away. The conversation kicks into high gear then, because although you both speak English fluently, there's something so freeing about talking with someone in your native tongue.

When he asks if you'd like to walk with him the next day, you say you'd love to but don't want to slow him down. You're nursing blisters on your feet and have one ankle wrapped. He says that's okay, that he's ready for an easy day.

The next morning you patch up your feet and wrap your ankle with special care, and it seems to help because you're hardly bothered by them all day. But you realize that you're walking well because you're falling in love, and the only thing you're paying attention to is this wonderful man and the flutter in your belly. You walk farther than you would have on your own, twenty-four kilometers into Estella, and you laugh when he still refers to it as an easy day. Subtle mention has been made about how sometimes it's nice to get away from the crowds in albergues. The two of you go to a hotel.

The next morning, you have no idea how much you slept and you don't care. Your time in bed together stretches into mid-morning, and you enjoy breakfast and finally leave town hours behind the crowd you usually see on the trail. In spite of the late start, you walk as far as Los Arcos, a distance of twenty-one kilometers and there find another hotel room. He takes you out for a special dinner, and you wear a light dress that, until you met him, you thought had been a mistake to pack.

Your feet, under the dinner table, are throbbing, and you know you've overdone it. When you mention the pain and say you need a really short day tomorrow, he squirms.

You wake in the morning to see him sitting on the edge of the bed. He smiles as he suggests the two of you get an earlier start than yesterday, and your touches and kisses don't change his mind.

On the trail, you are limping. Sometimes he walks ahead, as if those long legs have a mind of their own. His body turns to wait for you, but his eyes are still looking forward along the path.

When you say you are sorry, but you'll have to stop in Viana after eighteen excruciating kilometers, he says that's a good idea, but he'll push on to Logroño, an additional ten kilometers. You are unable to reply. You know he has a time frame. You know he's on a budget. You know that if he gets that far ahead of you today, it will be even farther tomorrow and you won't see him again.

You exchange phone numbers and email addresses. As he leaves you in Viana, he holds you for a long minute. Then he looks you in the eyes and says, "Buen Camino, okay?"

♦ THREE ♦

You've suffered from chronic fatigue for thirty years. It was so bad that you spent several of those years in a wheelchair. You always set walking goals for yourself, but there were days when walking thirty to forty meters, about seventy steps, would send you back to bed utterly exhausted.

You and your wife never gave up hope. You run a business together, and she's taken over your roles on your bad days, and you try to make it up to her on the good ones. She's the one who first heard about dietary remedies, and you give much credit to healthy eating and yearly cleansing fasts for your improvement.

Gradually, the distance you could walk increased until a three-to-five kilometer walk each day was doable, and you thought maybe that was all the progress you needed to make to live a satisfying life. Meanwhile, a few of your friends had done pilgrimages on the Camino de Santiago and you heard their stories. Suddenly walking the camino struck you as an essential ingredient of a satisfying life, and the possibility was all you could think about. Could I do it? Am I crazy to even consider it? When you went out for your daily walks, you felt as though there were an engine running inside you.

When spring came and you were still feeling fine, you told your wife that you were thinking about hiking the camino the following year. She put her hands on your face and must have felt the humming of the motor because she said, "No, do it this year."

This year? But the farthest you had walked so far was twelve kilometers. She didn't want to hear it. She sent you off to shop and pack.

You started near Bordeaux, just a one hour train ride from your home. For the first week you took it very easy, and you realized that you weren't seeing much of the scenery because you were focusing inward, looking for signs that your energy wouldn't last. But each evening as you stretched out on a bunk in an albergue, you looked forward to getting up the next day and doing it again.

By the time you crossed the border into Spain, you had trouble remembering yourself as a wheelchair-bound invalid. You were tan and muscular, you were walking twenty to twenty-five kilometers a day and, as you reported to your wife on the phone, getting choked up in the telling, you were able to walk, and keep up, for an hour or two at a time with other peregrinos, healthy peregrinos.

It's in the two days between Roncesvalles and Pamplona that you meet five men who, in a way, form a constellation around you that will traverse Spain in the coming month. There are the brothers from Penticton, British Columbia who, at the head and the foot of a big table at the local bar each evening, transform loose gatherings of peregrinos into parties of good friends. There's your fellow-countryman who, it turns out, knows one of the friends whose camino stories you relished. He understands exactly what you mean about those stories starting your engine. The constellation is completed by two gentlemen from Florence, one a professor of languages and the other a museum curator. In Pamplona, you all go to a tapas bar together, and you can't remember when you've had such a good time.

You've heard reports from peregrinos about seeing the same people for three or four days then losing track of them. But somehow your constellation hangs together. The brothers are fast hikers but take days off fairly often. You are the slowest, but you are steady. Almost every

154

day, you walk for a while with one or two of your new friends or run into them during evenings at the albergue or out on a plaza enjoying the street scene. They know about your health issues and encourage you when you need it. There's one occasion when the six of you walk within sight of each other all day, and you end up doing forty kilometers. You are stunned at your accomplishment. They buy you dinner that night.

Arriving alone in Santiago, you go to the pilgrim office, just around the corner from the cathedral and stand in line with many others to get your pilgrim certificate. The people who work there fill out hundreds of these forms every day, writing a Latinization of each pilgrim's name in the appropriate blank. They say "Congratulations" when handing the documents over, but you can tell it's just part of their routine.

You hang out in Santiago for a few days and do a day-trip to Finisterre on the local bus before it's time to head home to France on the ALSA bus. You run into all five of your buddies during this time, and they each ask to see your certificate, something you know they wouldn't ask anyone else. But somehow they accurately guess that you keep it with you. They know what deep pleasure it gives you to pull it out, to show it to them, to hear their admiring whistles, to shake their hands in both of yours.

◆ ◆ ◆

I'm kind of a hermit. I spend a lot of quality time alone. My husband is much the same, and we sometimes spend quality time alone together.

That's what our walk on the camino looked and felt like. Yes, we talked, but we also spent plenty of time side by side inside our own heads.

We passed by old hermitages all along the way. Those

typically crumbling structures would start conversations. What would it have been like to live there? Imagine how close to God one would feel living on top of that high bluff. Sheesh, look how far they had to go to get water! And in the 21st century, what can replace hermitages in providing places where loner-types can survive and thrive? The on-line world?

My husband and I are lucky to live a ways out of town with very few neighbors, so we can be hermits at home. For vacations, we often choose remote places, far from crowds.

When we started the camino, we were a bit shocked by the numbers of peregrinos on the trail. This was no quiet walk in the woods. It was exceedingly rare to look ahead or behind on the camino and not see quite a few others. But over time, we found the same comfort and pleasure in having those other peregrinos around us as we find in our usual style of walking together. It turns out that a whole bunch of pilgrims can have quality time alone together.

That said, time and kilometers went by the fastest on the day my husband and I walked and talked with two British doctors for most of the morning and then with a young structural engineer from Curaçao in the afternoon. I realized that conversation is like music in the way it can mess with time.

I learned that about music while driving long distances. I make up silly songs and ballads and wordless tunes, and the miles just fly by.

Talking has even greater musical complexity than my humble compositions. It has interesting phrasing and dynamics. Voices change pitch and volume, and they carry a little tune for a shorter or longer length of time. I rode on the waves of that music during this social day on the camino as if I were going down a river. But rather than propelling myself with rhythmic arm strokes or oar pulls, I was just floating, floating in an inner tube of good company.

I still was very tired when we reached Belorado late that afternoon, so my body was obviously working hard even while my mind drifted downstream. But it was a sweet kind of tiredness, like the kind felt after enjoying the sparkle of light on water all day.

After cleaning up and organizing our packs in the attractive albergue at the entrance to town, my husband and I followed the narrow road toward the old churches and the hilltop fortress we could see a few blocks further on. The centuries-old hostal and the Iglesia de Santa María next door with storks sitting on the bell tower had me scouting for good photo angles. Meanwhile, my husband walked to the far side of the church. Next thing I knew, he was reaching for my elbow and saying, "Come see this."

Windows and doors had been cut into the cliff face far above ground level. There was no obvious way to reach them. The back of the church was built into the mountain, so I assumed at first that passageways and rooms had been carved out. But then another idea occurred to me. A tall ladder could be set up to reach the door, and a prospective hermit could climb up to a sparsely furnished cave after which the ladder could be removed for a predetermined length of time. I thought about that scenario for a minute, imagined myself being that hermit, nodded and said,

"Cool."

My husband and I wandered on to the Plaza Mayor and enjoyed one of our favorite alone together things to do in Spain – watching children play. No kids had earphones plugged into their ears. No eyes were glued to hand-held devices. There was no frenetic energy of the sort you see when kids play with toys that have flashing lights and electronic noises. Toddlers chased pigeons and jumped up and down steps. Boys kicked balls among themselves, dreaming of being soccer stars. Girls played clapping games and walked hand-in-hand. Skateboarders, wagon-pullers and bike riders navigated their way safely around the scene.

Parents were relaxed, enjoying the opportunity to talk. The only time they interceded in the children's play was if a ball went into the street. There were no arguments among the young ones, no tears, no pouting. Everyone was included. Everyone was active. Everyone looked happy. We noticed other peregrinos watching, too. When they walked past our bench, they commented that they wished childhood looked like this in their home countries. We agreed.

Really, it's hard for me to think of my camino in social terms. I didn't talk much and didn't spend more than a few hours with anyone except my husband. But the flow of people around me, the music of conversations, and the pleasure of watching kids and families interact made for an intense feeling of connection to humanity. I can imagine hermits in their caves or on their mountaintops communing with God but sometimes hearing the voice of the divine down below in the sounds of people being with people.

THE LAY DOWN YOUR
BURDEN CAMINO

♦ ONE ♦

Your sister has multiple sclerosis. You take her shopping, take her places just for fun, take her to the doctor's every week. You travel with her, even across oceans, to see other doctors who might be able to provide her with a new treatment. You fulfill all caretaking roles since you and she are the only members left in your family. You hold hope and worry and fear and frustration in equal measure within you at all times. You are so tired.

You're walking the camino for her, but you are relieved to be alone. You've hired someone to be with her for these weeks. You use your body to the point of exhaustion and pain so that she might be spared some. You enter several churches a day and light candles for her. The prayers are wordless but involve focused channeling of healing energy in a northwesterly direction, which is where she is in relation to Spain.

You come upon a shrine to Mary, mother of Jesus, tucked into the forest, and suddenly you have no idea where you started walking this morning or where you will end up this evening. It feels like a peaceful middle of nowhere, as if the shrine had been lowered from heaven.

You're ready for a break so you slip off your pack, get out your water bottle and an apple, and you sit in front of the statue of the Virgin. There are no candles here of course, but as you eat and drink you feel that you should offer her something. You look around for rocks or flowers or pine cones, but those don't seem like the right gift. Then you glance up at Mary's face, and she's looking into your eyes. You can tell she's seen it all and understands your struggle. So you offer her your sister and you know, then and there, that Mother Mary will care for her for the rest of her life.

♦ TWO ♦

At least twice a year, depending on how much time off you can get, you fly from the Netherlands to Spain to walk a section of the camino. You keep to yourself mostly, often hiking in the off-season, staying in the smaller albergues, starting out in the morning ahead of, or behind, the crowd.

When you do fall into conversation with other peregrinos, they are soon impressed by your familiarity with the trail and ply you with questions about weather, about languages (you are fluent in five of them), about different branches of the camino (you love the one that starts in southern Spain), about foods. When questions start to veer toward the personal, you have certain lines that you toss out.

"I hate to walk" is one that sets people laughing and seems so incongruous that it tends to divert the conversation. But if someone latches on to what you just said and asks why you do the camino if you hate to walk, you laugh again and say, "Penitence" with a shrug.

That takes care of it. What are they going to say after that? Ask if you murdered someone?

You chose that answer with care, and maybe they catch it and maybe they don't. No, if you had murdered someone and felt you had to suffer in reparation, that would be penance. Penitence is about being remorseful. You are, and you have been for all of the seven years that you've been walking the camino.

But as you walk, you've noticed that your sins don't stay put. They become dislodged and shift around. It mostly happens when you walk across the meseta. The first time you crossed it, you hated the landscape – so boring, so ugly. It could have been a true penance, if that's what you had been looking for, because you felt sorry for yourself every step of the 180 kilometers between Burgos and León.

The second time you walked across, you felt sad, and not for yourself this time but for the land and the ways that humans have disrespected it – by cutting down the forests, erecting huge skeletal electric power poles, by pushing around the fertile earth to make fake hills for overpasses. The wide horizons would be bearable if they weren't so rudely interrupted. You ask yourself why we don't appreciate things, places, and yes, even people, for what they are. Why do we get the urge to change them?

The third time, you realized that the meseta is a good place to think, because there is nothing to distract you. You thought about love and the unloving actions that happen anyway. You thought about forgiveness and why it's so much easier to forgive others than it is to forgive yourself.

This time, as you cross the high plain, the wheat is waving golden in the wind, and you feel like you're crossing an ocean. Nothing is required of you here but rhythmic movement and even breathing. You make your way, for hours it seems, toward the steeple you see on the horizon before you finally stand at the lip of the valley, looking down on the old village church. You sit on a shaded bench in its front courtyard, rest there on God's island, washed clean by the waves, emptied by the emptiness, eyes opened to the beauty all around.

♦ THREE ♦

You've never understood angst. What's with guilt and beating yourself up? We're all just doing the best we can, you reason. So you find it easy to cut yourself, and others, some slack.

When you were a kid your parents always said to put a happy face on things. And it wasn't just them. The whole immigrant community was like that. You knew bad things had happened in their home country. It was even part of history lessons at school. But once your folks were in North America, they didn't want to dwell on the past or talk about it, at least not in the presence of the younger generation.

Your forty years of life have been pretty easy-going so far – no major deaths, no family dysfunction to speak of, no bad screw-ups. You're not married, but the long-term relationships you've had have ended fairly amicably. Your partners said that you glossed over things, that you weren't willing to hash out the hard stuff. "What hard stuff?" you said.

On the camino, you expected peacefulness, friendliness, and good cheer, and those things are present in abundance. But there's also hard stuff, and that you didn't expect.

In Roncevalles, you went into the cathedral to look around, and pacing back in forth in front of the altar was a young couple. The man was holding a very still and quiet baby against his chest. He and the woman were whispering urgent prayers.

On the plaza in Navarette, you met a man from Switzerland doing the camino on a bike he can pedal with his arms. He has an auto-immune disease that has robbed him of control of his legs and, within the next few years, the rest of his body will follow suit.

And early one sunny morning in the countryside of Galicia, an old woman herding her eight sheep approached you on the camino. When she saw you, she quickly pulled a small umbrella out of her shoulder bag and snapped it open at such an angle that her face would be hidden from your view. But you got a glimpse of terrible scarring.

Now you're in Santiago de Compostela attending the pilgrims' mass at the cathedral. They're not swinging the big incense burner today, so the group that gathers in the side pews is fairly small. The helpers hand out programs that include the prayers, readings and explanations of what will happen written both in Spanish and in your native language. They also hand each person a 3" by 5" piece of stiff black cardboard.

After the soft-spoken and gentle-eyed priest welcomes everyone, he ushers the group to a colonnaded courtyard. He holds up a piece of the black paper and, as he explains its purpose in Spanish, you find the corresponding place in your program. It represents your selfishness. You hear him say this simply and without judgment.

Selfishness is not a trait you've given much thought to, not since you were a kid and were learning to share. But the word gives you pause, makes you want to reframe some of your assumptions about who you are.

The priest then starts a fire in a metal brazier on the ground and invites everyone, his eyes meeting each participant's briefly, to place their cardboard into the flames, to give up their selfishness.

And just as your piece of stiff black paper is transformed, in a flash, to wispy gray ash, so something rigid in you disintegrates and flutters away on your next few exhalations. You feel as though there's a beam of light in your chest.

◆ ◆ ◆

I'm a teacher. I'm efficient and hard-working. I'm mostly vegetarian. I'm a tap dancer. I'm a strong woman. I'm a multi-tasker. I'm a gardener. I'm a wife. I'm a mother.

I spent decades investing time, and sometimes money, in becoming these things. Having words to define myself felt really important.

Then I loaded up my pack, put on my boots and started walking the camino. I was one walker among hundreds, and all of the labels that I figured were attached to me were nowhere to be seen. Like the proverbial house of cards, something so insubstantial was bound to fall.

On the camino, we were all just peregrinos. Oh, sometimes in conversation, we'd mention what kind of work we do back home, but it didn't seem important. It was so far away. Mostly talk was about what was happening that very day with perhaps a short reference to yesterday. Even that was a stretch. I had quickly realized that if I didn't write down, each evening, where I had been, what I had seen, what I had eaten, who I'd met and how I'd felt, those details would be gone. Was my memory on the blink? It was a little scary.

But it was also kind of blissful. With all those label cards knocked down, details and memories had no walls to bounce off of or to contain them. There was just a lot of open empty space, and open space is wonderful for stretching out your arms and twirling.

Some of the labels I had attached to myself were stickier than others, and I had to give some thought to them. Like the strong woman label. Except for the first year of my life, when my mother said I seemed happy to just sit and look around, I've always been active. As a kid I was competitive and wanted to jump higher, run faster, kick a ball farther and do more sit-ups than others. By the time I was in college, I soured on competition but took up long-distance bike-riding and training in ballet and modern dance.

Inevitably, age took its toll. But I was shocked when I started hiking the camino by how many physical problems I was having. I felt anything but strong. Luckily my husband was there to provide some perspective. "Yes, but you're doing it. You're hiking to Santiago," he'd say. So heck, I must still be strong, but I'm also not strong, I thought, and this was a revelation. I didn't have to be one thing or the other. I could be both, even though they seem to be opposites.

The other label I thought about was the "mostly vegetarian" one. Okay, it already sounds wishy-washy, I know. Finding a way of eating that works to satisfy my moral scruples as well as health needs and social needs has involved some compromise.

In a nutshell, (ooh, that sounds vegetarian!) I don't buy meat at the store, because I find some practices of the North American meat industry objectionable. At restaurants and friends' houses, I'll occasionally eat chicken or fish (and turkey on Thanksgiving) because otherwise there might be very little to eat or I might be asking too much of cooks who don't have experience making meatless meals. My husband and I live in the north, so once a year he hunts for one moose or two caribou. He eats most of the meat because, besides my meat industry considerations (which do not apply to his very respectful hunting practices), my body just feels and functions better without meat.

So what do I do on the camino when the pilgrim menu does not include choices for first and second courses, and one or both include meat? Well, I eat it. The small bits of melt-in-your-mouth pork in the Galician stew or of ground beef in the spaghetti sauce probably came from a farm within walking distance of the eatery and from animals that were not pumped full of hormones or medications. Seeing the restaurant cook walk into her kitchen with a big bucket of freshly-peeled potatoes, seeing small white trucks delivering fresh bread to the doors of homes and bars, seeing the same green vegetables in the soup that I identify in the gardens, seeing small colorful fishing boats in Spanish harbors, and hearing everywhere the unmistakable squawk of hens laying eggs, let me know that the food I was being offered was fresh from the earth that I'd watched being tended so lovingly. A sacred connection between the eater and what is eaten is more important to me than cognitive distinctions about "I eat this, and I don't eat that."

So once the labels I'd attached to myself became irrelevant, what was left? Just me -- walking, eating, sleeping, stretching, writing notes, looking, listening. Why make things complicated? I didn't have to be anything particular, and that meant I could just be.

THE NEVER-ENDING CAMINO

♦ ONE ♦

The two of you have been avid hikers throughout your almost fifty-year marriage. You say, only half-jokingly, that if you hadn't spent a lot of time walking together, you would have driven each other crazy. You also like to joke about how your two sets of legs start each hike looking as good as fifty-five year old legs. Then, a few weeks later, you check each other out and declare the strong legs you see to be not a day over thirty-five. Seriously though, you feel blessed to have stayed fit so long.

You moved to the Toronto area from the Netherlands twenty years ago for professional reasons, and you've done some wonderful hiking in North America on the Appalachian Trail and on the Gaspé Peninsula. But your favorite hikes have been in Europe. There's something about walking the land you grew up on. It's as though the topography is in your bones.

The Camino de Santiago is the first pilgrimage trail you've ever hiked. It's a very different experience. In fact the two of you don't talk about hiking it; you talk about walking it. Even though it is a long trail,

168

and quite rugged in places, it never seems like a challenge to be conquered but a mission to be embraced.

You started the camino three years ago from the doorstep of your old home near Amsterdam. Your daughter and her family live there now. Even as you waved goodbye from the street, she was still calling after you, "Wouldn't you like a lift out of town?"

That first summer, you walked through your home country, then Belgium, and into northern France. The second year you started where you'd left off the previous summer and thought you would walk as far as St. Jean Pied-de-Port, but realized it made more sense to walk the hard day over the Pyrenees when you both had your thirty-five year old legs at the end of a hiking season, rather than at the beginning of the next year. So you ended that year in Roncesvalles, just across the border of Spain.

In late April of year three, you flew from Canada to Madrid, then took train and bus to Roncesvalles and began, once again, the pleasurable experience of putting one foot in front of the other. Even though you see many more peregrinos along the trail here in Spain than you did the previous two summers farther north, and the social atmosphere is much livelier, the difference between a recreational trail and a pilgrimage trail still is evident to you. The act of walking the camino is ripe with meaning, and everyone you meet becomes a poet trying to find the right words to describe what they're feeling. The way you've found to express it is to say that the camino is not just a horizontal path across the surface of the planet, but is also a journey that goes deep down to your core.

A week before you reached Santiago, you and your husband discussed whether it was time to make train reservations to get from Spain to the Netherlands to visit your family. Eurail has gotten so crowded that the sooner one books seats, the better. But you decided to hold off for a while. You thought you might want to continue on to Finisterre.

Sure enough, you both were up for the additional ninety kilometers to the coast. You figured it would take three or four days to get there, after which taking a few days to enjoy the beach sounded appealing. Again you asked yourselves if it might be a good idea to go ahead and make those train bookings. Still you held off.

Now in Finisterre, you sit at an outside table enjoying an afternoon coffee and writing postcards. Some fellow peregrinos stop by and ask about your plans. You say you'll rest a few days, then walk north along the coast to Muxía, where the Virgin Mary was said to have arrived in a stone ship to encourage the apostle James when he became discouraged about his missionary work in Spain. From there, the trail is a loop heading back toward Santiago. "Sounds like a lovely walk. Buen Camino," they say. You've never grown tired of hearing those Spanish words through this entire leg of your three year camino. Meanwhile, you and your husband agree that one of these days soon, you'll need to make those train reservations. But not quite yet.

♦ TWO ♦

Like so many others, you started your camino in St. Jean Pied-de-Port. Like so many others, you counted down the approximately 800 kilometers you would walk to reach Santiago de Compostela.

But unlike many others, your physical well-being has improved along the way. Your early blisters disappeared, never to recur, and your tight upper back and stiff knee relaxed and caused you no more trouble. Your pack feels like part of your body now, and your feet feel strong and supported inside your boots. Steep uphills and downhills, hurdles in the minds of some peregrinos you've spoken with, are thrilling to you like the big ocean waves that you love to surf.

Your plan had been, after graduation ceremonies and family gatherings were behind you, to hike to Santiago and then fly home to start a job search. But you called your parents two weeks ago from Santiago to let them know your return would be delayed, that you wanted to continue walking for more of the summer. Your dad seemed to understand. Your mother definitely didn't. Sometimes you think she has a mental checklist of things that have to be accomplished in a certain order and at a certain time. You know you frustrate her, but you can't help it.

You continued on to Finisterre, stood on the cape looking out over the Atlantic, and thought of all the wonderful things you'd experienced along the route. You thought about how you'd like to see the corn and sunflowers grown tall over your head instead of only knee high as they were on your way west, how you'd like to feel the summer heat on the meseta, how you'd like to stand again on some of the high ridges you crossed in the fog, but with clear skies and long views this time. You thought of all the albergues where it would be a pleasure to stay again and those for which you would seek an alternative should you find yourself late in the day in certain towns. You turned your body so that your back was to the ocean, and there were all those dreams -- right in front of your feet.

So you washed your clothes, aired your boots, bought small tubes of sunscreen and toothpaste and headed east, retracing your steps. Sometimes it's been tricky at intersections, when no westbound peregrinos are in sight, to determine which way to go. In those instances, you try one of the options and then look back to see if camino markers are visible. You've usually gotten it right. You think maybe the camino has an aura.

You have a vision of yourself, weeks from now, crossing the border into France, entering St. Jean Pied-de-Port and buying the maps you'll need to continue on through France and Germany. You want to walk all the way home.

Peregrinos heading to Santiago do a double-take when they see you walking toward them. But it's clear that their confusion quickly changes to realization and a bit of awe. Wow, someone walking back the other way!

They say "¡Hola. Buen Camino!" warmly, and you nod and mumble something in return. You find it hard to meet their gazes because you can feel fire shining in your eyes. You don't want to freak anyone out, and you also don't particularly want to share the fire with anyone. The one person you will look at directly will be your mother when you cross the threshold of your home some months from now. You want her to see it in your eyes, want her to realize that although it's not something on her checklist, the fire is something to celebrate, something for which she should be proud of her son.

♦ THREE ♦

When your husband retired from his engineering position at the textile plant, your parents were still alive and living in the small apartment at the rear of your house. Your days, at that point, remained much the same as they had always been -- filled with the work of maintaining your home, caring for your mother and father who had gotten frailer with each passing year, and walking to town to swim, do the shopping, or stop by your daughter's hair salon or your son's dental office to see if either had time to join you for coffee. They are so busy with their own lives.

Your husband, however, bought an RV and lots of maps and tourist guides to various regions of Europe. He started planning excursions -- day tours, weekend outings, and week-long camp stays. After your parents passed away, you and your husband moved your best stuff into the small apartment that had been theirs, found good renters for the house, and travelled more.

You came to love the RV. It's so easy to clean, and it forces you to keep life simple. No clutter. Now, the two of you have started thinking about renting out the apartment as well and just living out of the RV. You made the point that it would be important to camp in places where it is inviting to go out for walks. Otherwise, you'd both feel too cooped up.

That's when your husband pulled the guidebook about the Camino de Santiago from his box of travel reference materials. It was different than the others in the box, which were more along the lines of resorts, spas, and historical sites. He shrugged as he opened it up, said it somehow had intrigued him. He suggested that the two of you motor along the route and get out and walk parts of it when you felt like it. A shiver ran up your back. You hadn't gotten so excited about an idea in a long time.

You bought some Spanish grammar books and language CDs, and the two of you set aside time each evening for study. Your husband stocked up on art supplies and transferred a lot of old photos off the hard drive of his laptop to make room for camino pictures.

You decided to just stick with RVing and walking within Spain. There are several branches of the camino within the country that can keep you busy for a long time and maximize the benefits of your Spanish studies. After walking the Camino francés, you can do the northern route along the coast, the southern route from Sevilla, and shorter branches from Somport, Oveido, and northern Portugal. The RV gives you such flexibility.

After the long drive from your home in Warsaw, you finally found yourself at the border of Spain just up the road from St. Jean Pied-de-

Port. Your husband pulled over at the large sign that said "Welcome to Navarre" in Spanish and Basque. You got out, and he said he would drive to Valcarlos, park the vehicle someplace where the two of you could spend the night, then walk back down the road to meet you.

And some variation of that plan has worked out for every day's venture. He either walks part of the way with you in the morning then returns to the camper, or he drives out in the morning and meets you somewhere in the early afternoon.

In between times, he photographs and draws and paints. He enjoys chatting with the bar owners when he stops somewhere for coffee. He learns a lot about the area that way and surprises you with the small out-of-the-way restaurants, churches, and museums he's discovered. You've never seen him so content.

And you are walking the camino – about ten to fifteen kilometers a day, carrying just your rain jacket, water, a piece of fruit, and blister pads. Everyone passes you, and you don't mind at all. They still have so much life ahead of them, you understand, that the trail pulls them forward to meet it. You on the other hand are happy for each uncomplicated day, in your simple RV, in the easy company of your husband. This, really, is all you want to do for the rest of your life.

◆ ◆ ◆

I wasn't ready for my camino to end in Santiago de Compostela, partly because my husband and I had taken the bus across the middle of Spain, partly because physically I was doing relatively well, partly because I was in love with Galicia and wanted to see more, and partly because where the land meets the water is a more natural ending point than a cathedral for an earth-lover like me.

By Finisterre, though, I felt ready for the walking part of the camino to be at an end. I ceremoniously placed my falling-apart hiking boots into the dumpster outside the small beach-side hotel where we spent one night. But there was another, more important, aspect of the camino that I wished would never end – the part where I felt such peacefulness. I was concerned that I might lose that when my feet left Spanish soil.

Within forty-eight hours, I was to find out. From Finisterre, we took the bus back to Santiago. There, we visited the peregrino museum, which had been closed on the day of our previous stay in the city, and went shopping for the one souvenir we felt we must have – a royal blue tile with a golden scallop shell on it like the ones which had guided our way for the past month.

The next morning, we hoisted our packs and walked to the ALSA bus station for the twenty-four hour ride to Paris. We'd had a few lovely days in Paris about fifteen years prior and had always said we'd like to go back. Other peregrinos were on the bus, so at first there was a sense of camino camaraderie as we shared stories during meals and breaks. But one by one they left the bus, locals got on, and my husband and I, each about six feet tall, felt utterly squished as we tried to get some sleep in a bus designed for shorter Spaniards, for maximum profits, or both.

We arrived in Paris on a Sunday morning, and the crowds were intense. We checked into a hotel near the Bastille, as we had fifteen years earlier, and walked for hours revisiting favorite sites. At the end of the day, we were tired and overwhelmed by the bustle and noise. We probably would have just headed to the train station to escape at that point if we had not already booked two nights at the hotel. We realized that sleeping in a bed would probably ease our stress and lift our moods.

Sure enough, Monday saw a quieter, less crowded city, and we found a small art museum tucked into the Tuileries that was a visual treasure chest. Heading back toward our hotel afterward, we happened to walk on the opposite side of the Rue de Rivoli than our usual one. We approached a wrought-iron gate that led into a lush garden, a zone of tranquility along the busy boulevard. Entering, we were delighted to see the square stone tower that we had wondered about from a distance. We stood before the interpretive sign, reading slowly with our limited French, and soon we were grinning from ear to ear, and ear to ear. This was the Tour St. Jacques, the Tower of St. James, where pilgrims congregated during the Middle Ages to journey to Santiago. We were back! We were still on the camino!

The following day, we made our way via train and bus to Mont St. Michel on the coast northwest of Paris, a historic site we had always wanted to visit. In the stark and maze-like abbey at the peak of the hill, the scallop shell symbol was everywhere. The Mont was a pilgrimage destination for many who couldn't afford, or who hadn't the health, to make it to a more distant holy place like Santiago, Rome or Jerusalem. I struggled to imagine the children's pilgrimages of the 14th to 18th centuries, when kids as young as eight left home and family to walk for months or years in order to ask for the blessing of a saint. How desperate their lives must have been!

As we left the abbey, we paused to browse in the gift shop. Among the many books there, we saw some about the

Camino de Santiago available in several languages. A man and his traveling companions were pouring over one, and I told them we had just completed the pilgrimage trail. The man's eyes sparkled when he replied that he had done the camino six years ago. Then he looked down at our beat-up sandals and chuckled in recognition of peregrino footwear.

The final leg of my husband's and my journey was to visit his parents in west-central Germany. In years past, we had seen scallop shell markers in his home town since, historically, it was the site of one of the very few bridges across the Ruhr River and was therefore a key link in the pilgrimage route from Germany heading toward France. We planned to take some walks, during our visit, along this segment of the camino.

But the best surprise was yet to come. On our first afternoon there, we ambled along the cobblestoned pedestrian zone through the old part of town and saw something ahead, something that hadn't been there on our last visit. People were standing around it, checking it out. As we drew nearer, we saw that it was a rough-cut rectangular stone plinth, about seven feet tall. On the side facing us, we read, "Santiago de Compostela – 2,667 kilometers." We laughed with sheer amazement at the synchronicity of it all. It had just been erected two days before our arrival. Each side of the column had different pilgrimage symbols on its face – a scallop shell, a walking stick, the cathedral of St. James. One man nearby was raising a fuss about it. "Some car will just come along and run into it," he exclaimed in German. "It's in the way!"

We had fun each day, during outings, sauntering by to listen to what people had to say about it. Except for that one irate man, everyone else loved it and felt honored that their town was taking part in the restoration of the pilgrimage route.

At home a few weeks later, my husband carved a six by six inch square out of the rounded surface of one of the larger timbers by the door of our log home. I mounted the blue and gold scallop shell tile into it. Each time I go in or out the door, I am on the camino. When I go out for walks, sometimes my brain leaves the trail I am actually walking and takes me back to Spain. When I am at work, I find that the calm acceptance I found on the camino is still alive and well.

And when my husband and I talk about travelling plans for the next few years, we first plug family visits into the calendar. But I've already bought new hiking boots, and I'm seeing a physio to learn ways to improve the workings of my knees and feet. We are determined to walk the camino again. I can hardly wait! And who knows? Maybe I will see you and you and you there.

ABOUT THE AUTHOR

Dianne Homan lives off-grid in a log cabin with her husband, and hiking buddy, in the Yukon Territory of northern Canada. She walks a camino every two years or so.

Made in the USA
Lexington, KY
06 May 2017